A Dialog in My Abyss

A Dialog in My Abyss

Domingo Franco

Library of Congress Control Number:		2011933279
ISBN:	Hardcover	978-1-4633-0487-4
	Softcover	978-1-4633-0489-8
	EBook	978-1-4633-0488-1

This book was printed in the United States of America.

To order additional copies of this book, contact:
Palibrio
1-877-407-5847
www.Palibrio.com
ordenes@palibrio.com
356060

CONTENTS

DEDICATIONS

To the memory of my parents: Domingo Franco Sánchez and Dolores Assad Rivera, for whom I applied the entire strength of my spirit not to be acknowledged by them as a severely depressed man. During this time I considered that the best approach consisted of preventing them from the sorrow of the woes that afflicted me. I strongly, and prejudicially, believed that a mentally ill man was finished and had no remedy; with the same detriment that is used to point out a thief who has been discovered and exhibited to society.

To my wife: Maria de la Paz Hernández Orozco, from whom I have received her comprehension, joy of life and the needed impulse that convinced me to seek psychiatric treatment. Likewise, for the important moral support that I have always received from her during complicated days.

To my brothers: Maria Guadalupe, Leticia, Sonia, Rafael and Salvador, in whom I always receive support and happiness whenever we are together.

INTRODUCTION

It is commonly accepted, amongst modern researchers, the idea that if certain knowledge is not questionable, it is simply because it is not in a field of science. History teaches us that the explanations of science are not ultimate since they are subject to many corrections or theses that disprove their version. This same process allows us to advance in the degree of certainty of that which is studied. But this does not inevitably deny that all past philosophers were wrong, and that they should not be taken into account for recent axioms or proposals.

As an example we have the concrete case of the inventor of logic, Aristotle, whose ideas remained captured throughout the centuries. Great thinkers, from 280 BC all through the past 20th century, harvested and fertilized these ideas. As much as others have objectified them, they are valid in modern symbolic logic, or mathematical logic, or logistics; that attempt of deductive processes is applicable to mathematics or any other scientific field. Through a language of mostly rigorous symbols it reaches our days with a profile of an instrument used to develop, support and criticize mathematics. The connection point with Aristotelian logic prevails in the structure of thought and its deductive rules.

Also the Greek philosopher Democritus of Abdera, who in the 5th century BC formulated the theory of the atomists, where he considered that reality was composed of two types of unique elements: a void and atoms. He held that these particles moved perpetually in empty space, and according to its shape and size, constituted the different state of physical bodies. In opposition to twenty five centuries of obscurity, a new zenith returned in the 17th century AD with the ratification of the atomic energy hypothesis.

And for those who today wish to study the mechanics of fluids, does not it begin with "the principle of floating bodies"? In another part of physics is it not still taught, due its usefulness, "the equilibrium of planes"? These were initially formulated by the Greek erudite Archimedes of Syracuse in the 3rd century AD. Likewise, many more men of antiquity devoted to science, art, philosophy, politics, etc., and we continue serving ourselves from their legacy. In all, the less that we know about the past, the less we would take advantage of the treasures that history reserves for us. Astoundingly, not only an erudite researcher finds them, they are still for he who, with no reservations, sets to find them.

This is the starting point of my investigation, the harbor were I set to sea to explore the immense ocean of my fears and confusions, that made themselves feel relentless by depression; an illness that I moderately suffered from since I was twenty four years old, but that I resented mercilessly before I was thirty.

I do not doubt that probably due to my ignorance, I did not find refuge in modern psychology. Instead, in that which regardless of being purely archaic to many, for me, far from that, are powerful foundations that have remained surprisingly as unaltered as spurned. It could have been due to the habit of always looking at the past, or for being simply quixotic, or for another reason that I do not recognize; it is the case that with the fervor of someone who begs for forgiveness during torment, and with the faith of whom the truth is surely known. I moored during the worst times of my life, gambling my future completely, to the reflections that some have called the awakening of moral science; the then and now of the history of universal philosophy.

CHAPTER I

The Meeting

M uch like the sea that is propelled by the consequences of a natural force, suddenly it leaves the coast to return, leaving more devastation in its path. This is how I see myself, surrounded by agitated waters without knowing how or why I find myself here. I would like it to be a nightmare, although I know perfectly well that it is not. I float in a dark and isolated ocean; it seems to be inside an inferno, a terrible inferno that, in some way, exists inside us and in certain part of our soul. I do not know if many know it, because in life they are exclusively reserved for deranged souls. These are places destined to undergo abrasive anxieties. It is not necessary to cross a door— just like Dante describes—in which it is inscribed in letters of fire: "Abandon hope all ye who enter here". Likewise, the threat of the eternal guardian of the gates of hell, Cerberus—the three headed dog—is not needed. From here where? Is perhaps the most terrible question I have had to endure. Will this silent storm remain forever, in superb swing waves, in obscurity, alone? I do not feel the change, not even with the promises of death itself. I would not want for anyone to join me, since there is no one that I would wish so much suffering onto, and I do not believe that there is anyone that could help me. Being far away by its intensity, I have limited strength to stay afloat. There are without a doubt moments of calm, spaces of little agitation, periods of physical and spiritual breathing, during which I wonder if fortune will grant me an open road. My spirit fights solely through the hope and resilience that fortune holds for me. Also by a passion that, without a doubt, was obtained from formed ideals inspired by epic feats. There should be some purpose, I ask myself, due to the fact that these stories, of noble historical acts, reached my hands and created such a big impression. Without a doubt, questioning with denoted egotism and exacerbated vanity I really no dot care for during this state. I gladly accept strength regardless of where it comes from. I know that with another fairy I would not have endured so many attacks, which are comparable to merciless spirits who madly pursue their victim, and whom they are obsessed to defeat; simulating an enchanting snake that drips from my defenseless and paralyzed body, poisoning my already mad thoughts and planting the idea of taking my own life. Perhaps it is due to my faith and the purpose to endure to the last blow, or by the terror of eternity, that I have luckily remained alive.

There are no stars; the universe itself is bolted down by obscurity and, with that, the absolute hopelessness of someone who is losing a decisive battle. There is no wonder why it is called dark Tartarus! I continue ahead over the water, as if I was a shipwrecked who is trying to save himself. However, I know that in this chaos one never reaches any destination. Does the direction that I am taking even matter? What place am I trying to reach? Why do I try? Again, I fall; so many battles in one day. To convince one's self is simple, it is a question of time, and no one can bear so much. It is precise to be dead than to endure the faith of Sisyphus—who was condemned to remain in hell, with the incessant punishment of having to push a rock up a hill and having it fall before reaching the summit.

My desperation uncontrollably augments. I ask myself, is this hell? The inconceivable anxiety where no one has found its end; the worst of the anxieties, "that which never ends". It is possible that we would have been created to always withstand the most intense torments.

Without making anyone a participant of my pain, with a wounded scream I implore to God that he has mercy on my soul. Listen to me and save me! O God my God! Opposed to the impossible I continue moving, even though it gets harder and harder to continue, as if a set of ghostly hands were holding my ankles. I loathe that which surrounds me. I loathe myself without excluding the uselessness of my strength. I feel exhausted. I will not stop; it is my only and most valuable purpose. If I am going to exceed it is because I will endure. This loneliness will serve to not transmit my tragedy to anyone; to not break the health or vitality of my loved ones!

If Leonidas was a soldier, surely his captains would order me to fight, telling me perhaps what they answered to the Great Xerxes—Persian emperor in charge of a never before seen army, due to its machinery and immensity, who before approaching a phalanx of Spartans that were trying to impede his path in the stretch of Thermopylae said: "Surrender, don't you understand that if I order it to be, this army that is watching you, will shoot their arrows at the same time with so many projectiles that they will hide the sun!"—Surprisingly, that small group of heroes replied: "Even better, this way we will fight in the shadows". Yes, it is better to die this way, in the midst of combat and with weapons in one's hand. Just like them, I will not stop! It is definite!

Slowly, exhaustion overtakes me. I cannot do it anymore, I recognize it; with everything I have, I will use the strength to the extent of my limitations. And if I was soldier from Alexander's phalanx, he would tell me with a jovial and strong voice: "Macedonians! Your valor disables you from abandoning your dominion; I will not give up my determination until we have obtained in these regions the victory that you are desperate for, or an honorable death. My lineage does not guarantee long life; instead I rely on my mythical name".

Nothing will stop me, I promise. In this dimension, Cronus does not interfere, like this, which man will endure? Again, just like voracious sharks that attack their prey, exhaustion and fear assail my will. The end of my life must be near. What a tragedy! I cannot continue! I am beat! Inexplicably I go on. Thoughtlessly, I am carried by the last reserves of strength that my soul has; available to those who are willing to survive beyond what is humanly possible. Christ, do not let me go!

Take my hand! Have compassion Lord! Have mercy my God!
How have I finished: lost without succession, or end, in the
waters of a great abyss.

Now I remember a beautiful dream, only one beautiful dream,
but hopeful nonetheless. It also took place in the sea: I was
floating and playing in its tranquil and sunny waters, when
suddenly I was attacked by voracious animals that were
ripping my flesh. I did nothing more than close my eyes with
all my strength and decided to die. I begged God to take my
poor soul, whilst my body was being violently shaken by the
ravenousness of the dogfish. Soon after, my osseous remains
plunged to the bottom of the sea, deposited with the gentleness
of the current. My soul, reluctant to detach itself from the
body, remained there; due to disconcert perhaps, or by the wait
of what is not constituted as having been a fatality. A short
moment later, something was sharply pushing my back; with
obligation I opened my eyes. I was scared to see my buried
remains; however, I was surprised to see in front of me an
enormous white dolphin whose head was pushing me with
the intention of wanting to wake me up. I then saw my body
intact, as if it all had been a dream within a dream. With the
relief of someone who wakes up from a terrible nightmare,
I approached, hugged and kissed it; with the gratitude of
someone who thanks life after being saved. Then, we emerged
with the effort of its membrane, and, without anxiously
wanting to breathe, I held onto his fin and we glided toward
the distant coast. It was so fast that I did not have the chance
to look back where the predators where.

Will these waters of nebulous atmosphere be what the ancient
Greeks used to call Stygian waters? Not much less than the
gloomy waters from hell. I am so beaten that I did not repair
the tenuous light in the horizon. I can barely see something
and this reanimates me a little. Now not everything is the sea

and the quiet shadows. Will it be an illusion? Or are there reliefs over the distant waters? Or have they perpetually been there? Regardless, there is hope. If I could only get close! Patience, patience, patience, it is necessary to endure. God allow me to come, do not let the current take me away. Every stroke seems like the final one, fear consumes my energy completely, it multiplies my exhaustion. Do not fool yourself, is what my inner voices tell me, the strength from your body has abandoned you. Without consciously accepting defeat, I did not know more until seeing myself at the shore, with the sensation of a soul reduced to the final emaciation.

It seems that I have finally arrived at a station, so somber that it could be the island of the dead. I will have to wait for the ferryman Charon—human figure, dressed in a white shroud, who is in charge of taking the souls of mortals to the place of no return, to the pale shadows of Avernus—will it be true that there are many calamities in hell, such as fear, death and frightening figures.

Before me, the ruins, I am reminded of what surrounds me; it seems to be besieged by abandonment. I suggest that it has been abandoned, just like one forgets about certain things that are no longer useful. Nothing incites my curiosity with more determination than the continuation of a walled path. Just like a bird that is fascinated by the sight of a serpent. It makes me feel attracted, perhaps by this wind that, by crossing its path, caresses me and then loses itself in that same trail. Engrossed and in a slow pace, I allow myself to be carried away by the pleasure of a brief rest, after a long, very long, pilgrimage. This sensation is experimented the deeper I go with each breath. Will it be possible that this is the attraction of the profound Orcus? To my rear, the sea and the shore, its limit, with me fear, and always in front of me, could it be by cowardice or courage, the yearning to live.

I imagine that this wall was the result of defensive work, perhaps the protector of strategic points for civilizations from antiquity, who just like the bellicose nations of today needed a military industry. Probably the spiritual sustenance of those men was the same as ours. We must have changed in something; the passions and cravings of the past will they be similar to those of now, or have only the objectives changed, who knows.

I could make out a fortified city, which shines by its own light against the immense grayness. Was this distant light, perhaps, what gave me this brief and incipient sense of hope? In the center an escarpment is seen, guarded by two marble porticos, which harmoniously stand along with other monuments and temples of equal beauty. The enchantment is so grand that, without taking my eyes from the august and artistic constructions, I remain engrossed. Its architecture captivates me. It is a bizarre sensation that ignites interest with each sculpture, which is seen from different angles with every step I take. They speak to my imagination and I search for the meaning of these majestic works. They even suggest to me that they do not belong to the mansion of saddened shadows, instead to the vast grounds of the Elysium.

I will rest for a brief moment here. Due to its decoration and levelness, it seems to be the main plaza. Why do I repeatedly think that this place guards a mystery that I incredibly like? Just like what fresh air would do if one is suffocating.

It is not possible to free myself from this whirlpool in my mind. It does not go away for a long period of time, because this immense solitude drowns me. Will I be paying an offense to God? Will I be dead? Will everyone be dead? Will I be part of what does not exist? I hope they let me rest so I can sleep a little. Without giving up, I feel that my head is surrendering to the weight of death. Without moving my lips, I hear the

whispering of my own voice: morning is not born from the
night, and nothing that is around you changes. If it was not
because of my sensibility and that murmur, I would have slept
through the dream of the voyage with no return. It could be
my drowsy view, or I barely see a silhouette that crosses the
plaza: they are vain ghosts. My heart is about to explode, it
is better for me to be calm, there are so many things that go
through one's mind in an instant; my fear of visions, indecision
and loneliness. I don't care what happens to me, I better
follow it, and I prefer it over loneliness. I am more terrified of
remaining in eternal silence, so I will walk at a prudent distance.
Overcome with fear and attentive to any change which will
force me to start my escape, I follow its path. It will leave if
I do not hurry. Why don't I catch up to it? No! I better not!
Predictably I do not have the guts!

Where will it go? Who will it be? I know that I cannot handle
the suspense, which is transforming itself into terror. It
violently penetrates, just like a sudden thrust that takes your
breath away. Euripides the poet once said, "When the gods
want to defeat a mortal, first they drive him mad". There
are now many streets, and I do not know if we have already
passed them or they are different ones, the point is that I cannot
continue distracted. It does not turn its head, perhaps by the
engrossment of its soliloquy. Finally it enters into a building,
it's a prison. Quickly it accelerates its pace, with the confidence
of someone who has surely found what he is looking for. Now
it stops in front of a cell, inside I see a man of old age with
a vulgar aspect, snub nosed, and robust complexion. He is
barefoot and dressed in a crude tunic. They greet one another.
I cannot talk or move, I am paralyzed. Slowly, my thoughts
become serene and my breath returns to its natural rhythm. I
hesitate to tell myself: "look at me, like at every stage of my
life! I have become an unhappy shadow of others", this is what
can be said about my subsistence in a few words, "A simple
shadow that does not deserve any repair"; a shadow that does

not dare to separate itself from friends of people who keep it company daily, because it does not have its own life, not even by the strength that is given by its ideals.

Should I get close? Enough with this cowardice! Always the same thing! No, please no! I do not even know if the shivering of my legs is because of my insecurities, or if my insecurities are the cause of my slimness. At last I decide to interrupt them, just like a traveler would ask for directions. I get near them and before any conjuncture, I see real men with the energy and material that nature provides to the living. Regardless of my presence, they pretend to ignore me, or truly they cannot see me. I am the ghost! Determined not to retreat, and motivated by an enigmatic breath, I wait. Meanwhile, my mind will allow me to abandon this terror and decipher what they are saying. Again, calling to their attention, I talk to them respectfully, without taking my eye from that rugged face, thick lips and popping eyes. I confirmed it as I see that my presence does not cause any reaction to any of them. Their dialog does not seem to be interrupted, or perturbed, by any distraction.

Incomprehensibly, a tranquil sensation gradually penetrates my soul, until I see myself free from impressions or fears. It is particular to me, after a moment of distraction I begin to listen to them, even in this state of relaxation that I hardly ever reach. At last, momentarily with the exception of my own persecution, I am able to maintain continuous and full concentration in their dialogue. It is my wish to partake; I have the eagerness to make inquiries. Perhaps through the lens of an anachronistic person, who has been granted to be in an epoch and place, where the events that were his source of inspiration stem from.

A Foreigner—Thank heavens that I find you still alive, today precisely when I so desperately need you. Help me! I am at the mercy of terror, it pursues me, and my torments are too big. It is truly insufferable! And I know that with your wise help I can fight these ills.

The Master—Remember that "If I am called wise is because those that listen to me believe that I know things that I discover from the ignorance of others. Only God is truly wise, and that precisely he has been trying to say through his oracle. Making it understandable that all wisdom is nothing great or better yet, that it's nothing. If the oracle has called me, then without a doubt it has used my name as an example, and he said it to men: the wisest amongst you is he who recognizes that his wisdom is insignificant. This is object of my indignations, and I continue doing it to assure myself more and to obey the God, serving as an interpreter; making the world see that no one is wise. This worried me so much that I did not have the opportunity to dedicate myself to the service of the republic, nor to any concerns of mine, but I am in utter poverty by reason of my devotion to God"[1]. "It is he who imposes the duty to help others to give birth; at the same time he does not permit me to produce anything. This is the reason why I am not the authority of wisdom, and why I cannot praise myself from any of my discoveries. As compensation, some of the people that converse with me show themselves to be very ignorant initially, but they make astonishing progress as our acquaintance ripens; they are surprised of this fruit, and it is because God wanted to fertilize them. It is ostensible that they have direly learned from me, but they made many of their findings on their own. I have not done much except contribute with the God to help them discover"[2]

---

[1]   Diálogos de Platón, Apología de Sócrates (Sócrates VS 556 Jueces)

[2]   Diálogos de Platón, Teetetes (O de la ciencia)

Take into account during every moment of our dialogue, that I do not have the art or gift to cure the ills of men. I am neither a fortune teller, medic, wizard nor medicine man. And my prayers are not any different from those of any other just man.

The Foreigner—But I have heard you say, "True philosophers prepare themselves to have strength and be bold; this virtue liberates men from their wants and fears, making them superior to their emotions and pleasures. And without it, those men that acquire strength obtain it as a result of fear. Or those that pretend to be moderate or bold do it by acting with intemperance; giving as a result a mad and ridiculous wisdom, since they renounce a pleasure they covet and face a fear that terrorizes them. This means that they defeat their emotions as a result of their interest in any of the passions that they are submitted to or that enthrall them. Becoming what you have said, moderate and bold by acting with intemperance"[3] Or have I not understood it properly?

The Master—You have understood it! "You do not have to be wrong, you do not walk towards wisdom substituting pleasures for pleasures, sadness for sadness, fears for fears, and doing the same than those who constantly switch coins; instead wisdom not seen as the omniscient knowledge, but as the thought of judgment. It is an authentic coin with which you can buy and have it all: strength, temperance, and justice. In one word, virtue is only true with knowledge, independent

---

[3]   Diálogos de Platón, Fedón o del alma (Sócrates vs. Simias)

*   Every year the Athenians would send a boat to the small island of Delos for a religious ritual dedicated to Apollo. When the epoch to verify it would arrive, the law stated that the city should stay pure and the death sentence should be prohibited until the ship arrived.

from all the pleasures, sadness, fears and the other passions. Whilst other virtues that appear from the transaction of certain passions with other, are shadows of virtue; slave virtue of vice, that does not have an apex of truth. The true virtue is a purification of the entire nature of the passions. Temperance, justice, strength and prudence are purifications; and there many signs that make us believe this. Those who established them were despicable characters, on the contrary, great geniuses who in my opinion have philosophized very well. I have not forgiven anyone for being of this type, and I have worked throughout my life to achieve it. If my efforts have not been short, and if I have achieved them, I hope to know it, with God's will, after the boat has returned from Delos*".

A Foreigner—For this reason I have been convinced that nature and the study of science has provided you with enough power to order ideas, with the goal to produce belief and give shape to your discourse. And that the crux of the influx of your magic consists of carrying organized and methodical discourses. "All who do not follow it are thrown into a dark path. However, he who follows it, will concisely explain the essence of the object whose words are being referred"[4] Should we not proceed in this manner, in the examinations that we make over the nature of each thing?

The Master—It is true what you say. It is agreed that we shall examine the nature of the things that we face. The first thing that we need to examine is that which is used as a subject or matter to the exercise of mental faculties, and that is not any other thing rather than what we propose; and that we want to penetrate, whether it's simple or convoluted. Then, if it is simple, what are its properties, how or over what does it have power on, and in which cases is it affected. If it is convoluted,

---

[4]   Diálogos de Platón, Fedro o del Amor

we will count the parts that can make it distinguishable, and over each one of them we shall reinitiate the examination to determine all the active and passive properties. According to this, and given that men have different personalities, complex and harmonious discourses shall be offered for those studious souls, and clear ones for the simple souls; therefore, it is necessary to make out those complex characters and utilize convoluted language, and a simpler tone for the rest. Also, it is important to speak always when it is opportune and to quiet also when it is convenient; which implies to employ and avoid the concise style.

A Foreigner—Then, with mercy, help me reach the benefit that virtue provides to fight my terrible ills; to be strong and sound against tragedies. Look at me, I have fallen in a state of sordid desperation. Are you not moved at the sight of a tormented man?

The Master—You do not need to implore to me for help, when really "I have as the worst: not wanting to help, even if it is myself, friends, relatives; therefore, today it is necessary to become strong and deal with the road that we are to travel"[5] But why is it that you want to begin our indignation?

A Foreigner—Undoubtedly because of all that it makes me fear.

The Master—Show me your resolution, "clearing and showing with moderation, leaving for later your affluent gifts. What is the fear and what is the objective that it should have? Such as that of a weaver and the making of garments"[5] Is this not what is happening?

A Foreigner—Yes

---

[5]—Gorgias o de la Retórica (Socrates VS. Callicles)

The Master—"And music, the composition of the melodies"[6]

A Foreigner—Yes. It is terrifying to apparitions and visions. Look, I knew that there were people that suffer of depression, and some are in extreme or critical conditions; these miserable beings are harassed by visions and voices, and whenever they are perturbed a grave pain is imprinted in them. This could be a fantastic torture given by their imagination; this and everything is real in their sentiments. Since I suffer from depression, I suppose that I could easily have one of these visions at any moment. And thinking about it thousands of times, I believe that the possibility seriously increases. Hence, I am certainly not a stranger to the suffering of the torments that the apparitions might provoke, from the instant that they stop being seen or heard; a trance that has become an unfaultable curse.

The Master—Does this mean that the apparitions or vision, and their voices, are something or nothing?

A Foreigner—If it is not in more than this, I will clarify to you that the apparition is the action and effect of manifestation, caused by a common change in mood.

The Master—By what you have said, do you fear all types of manifestations? Or only those that are only seen or heard?

A Foreigner—What a question! It seems bizarre coming from you. I would have thought it was mockery if it came from another, but I know you and I know that was not your intention.

---

[6]—Gorgias o de la Retórica (Socrates VS. Gorgias)

The Master—"If you are certain that you know me, you should note that you have not been able to handle what should be done with your present, as long as you do not answer the question"[7]

A Foreigner—I have noticed, that is why I am telling you, it is them that allow themselves to be seen or heard by me, exclusively.

The Master—Do you agree with me if I firmly say that, visions, are objects that relate to sight; they are real and are perceived initially by this organ, even when they can be objects represented by the mind. Perhaps, they are influenced by the gods and allow us to see the supernatural, whether they are real of inexistent.

A Foreigner—Completely.

The Master—And, employing similar language, does not it happen that, through the ear or mind or the will of the gods, we perceive voices or sounds of things that are real or inexistent?

A Foreigner—Entirely.

The Master—If I have understood correctly, you mainly fear any image perception or sound, which is feasible by the representations of the mind, or by the perceptions given by the power of the gods; or merely by the perception of objects and real sounds. Is this not correct?

A Foreigner—Oh God, are you trying to really help or drive me mad?

---

[7]—Gorgias o de la Retórica (Socrates VS. Callicles)

The Master—Simply for you to answer concisely what I have asked you.

A Foreigner—Of course I do not fear all the perceptions of sight or hearing. I fear those that can be seen or heard by fantasy or only imagination.

The Master—"Listen to me, it is not only with you that I proceed with this attitude every time I interrogate you for things that seem obvious, instead of guessing what is happening to you; in this style our dialog becomes strictly closer to the truth"[8]. How would you answer, is it not true that the mind of a mortal is designed to present the images of things that are real or ideal?

A Foreigner—Yes.

The Master—And those things can be objects that are not present?

A Foreigner—Yes.

The Master—Then, the mind has the virtue, or power, to invent or imagine with the objects that are not preset.

A Foreigner—Naturally.

The Master—Now, could to clarify to me what is it that you fear. I wish to understand it thoroughly. Is it casually common to invent or represent so many objects that are not present, such as ideal things? Is it such the power of imagination?

---

[8]—Gorgias o de la Retórica (Socrates VS Gorgias)

A Foreigner—No, have mercy! You have not understood me, note that I specifically fear visions and voices rather than what the industry of my imagination, or fantasy, display to me. It deals with a sound, object or image that is normally perceived by sight or hearing; of things that are real and tangible. My faculties of imagination or fantasy are not capable to voluntarily do it.

The Master—Then, you fear visions and voices that your fantasy and imagination produce, and are not products of the ordinary faculties of the mind? In sum, you do not fear any vision or voice that was previously perceived by sight or hearing, nor those that were commonly represented by the mind?

A Foreigner—Precisely.

The Master—Subsequently, if you do not fear any other apparition, no other will be terrifying, nor will it attract fear; neither real or fantasy. Will it not be like this?

A Foreigner—Well, not exactly. I recognize that supernatural apparitions are terrifying, especially those that come from fearsome abysses; as long as I knew that my imagination or fantasies did not recreate them.

The Master—Lastly, I conclude that you fear apparitions and voices that are represented by the mind, as if they were objectively perceived, but come from inexistent images and sounds; or negligible to the senses. Similarly, they are sensibly perceived by the supernatural forces of Hades. What else should we add or omit to be more exact?

A Foreigner—You have thoroughly understood me, and have shown with transparency what troubles me.

The Master—Have you ever thought that if we took out the sound from the voice, what should remain from it?

A Foreigner—Nothing, to say the least.

The Master—Is it not fundamental that the sound is the indispensable substance, better yet, the permanent and invariable part; the essence of voice?

A Foreigner—That is questionable.

The Master—Then, if we took out the voice from hallucination, or the sound from hell, what remains?

A Foreigner—Silence.

The Master—Moving along, it is not possible to fear these voices without their essence.

A Foreigner—I believe without repair.

The Master—What is your opinion vision? If we took out the faculty to perceive shapes and colors, what remains?

A Foreigner—Nothing

The Master—And said faculty is not an essence of vision?

A Foreigner—It is merely the essence.

The Master—For the same reason, it is impossible to fear visions without their shapes and colors.

A Foreigner—Yes

The Master—Likewise, if we took out forms and colors that the imagination represents from the apparitions, what would happen to them?

A Foreigner—The same as the voices without the sound.

The Master—And applied to the shapes and colors that ascend from the infernal bruises, will we denote that it is the exception?

A Foreigner—No, its personification would be impossible.

The Master—Also, is it impossible to fear these visions without their essence?

A Foreigner—Yes

The Master—Hence, only those sounds, shapes and colors trouble you much?

A Foreigner—Extremely.

The Master—Zeus! If the sounds, shapes and colors in each part are permanent, and invariable in each representation or sensible perception to the sight and hearing, how are those that trouble you different than the others? Given that you accept their horror, without having much to give; I cannot grasp an exact idea of what is happening to you. The case is that I do not accustom to have supposition understand what I have attempted to grasp.

"Perhaps I have misunderstood you my young friend, but this is precisely what motivates my stubbornness in proposing"[9]:

---

[9]—Gorgias o de la Retórica (Sócrates VS. Gorgias)

What particularity could the apparitions have, if at one point, they horrified you so much and analogous visions and voice do not? Or is the nature of said apparitions distinct with those of another voice or vision? Or perhaps, do these hallucinations, like the ones from hell, have the exclusivity to manifest sounds, shapes and colors?

It is perceived in the environment, in each breath, in his eyes, that silence does not accelerate any response; so it seems that it does not order them to give a reason to things. I am surprised at the fact that they do not wait for an explanation; neither the one that poses the question, nor the one that is trying to analyze it. I even begin to worry without hearing the obligated answer that I am accustomed to. Neither one demonstrates rivalry or the intention to triumph. They only look for one answer. They are really interested to investigate what is taking place. I ask myself: could it be the secret, what is inexorably demanded by the truth to open its doors?

A Foreigner—It is possible that under the fear I have, the real horror is hidden. How is it possible that I have not noticed? I now believe that nothing bothers me more than thinking that I could become mad.

CHAPTER II

Phobia to Madness

The Master—Observe that you are not being consistent with what I am asking you

A Foreigner—Make this clear?

The Master—Because I have just asked you if the essence of the voices and visions is unique or unknown. If this is the case, before inquiring, it is necessary to know what makes them different. Or, if the apparitions in question hold exclusive qualities, and to know how are they special.

A Foreigner—If they exist then I do not know them, and as far as special, how could they be expressed. In any case, I do not care much now, since I have discovered my authentic inferno. No, I do not find a better explanation to my fears rather than not wanting to go mad.

The Master—If this is what remains, we should not move away from the cause of the discussion, so we continue on our principal purpose. As long as we go on with the reflections and investigations to assure ourselves that the principles that we planted are exact; otherwise, our deductions or inductions will overwhelm us with rigor.

Show me what you call madness.

A Foreigner—I am satisfied with this definition: "when there is deprivation of reason and imprudent behavior, or perhaps, exultation of mood".

The Master—And the faculty of reason is something or is it nothing?

A Foreigner—Everyone knows that it is the quality through which man can imagine or judge. Where to imagine is to reflect.

It is to make a slow examination of something, which makes the soul and judgment of it inferred. Do you agree?

The Master—For now it is not my purpose to question your definition; therefore, we should leave this as a point of departure and go into this one: Do you agree that to submit ourselves to medics and their treatments is always a pleasant thing?

A Foreigner—Even with the developments of science, treatments, surgeries and procedures do not save us from suffering; even if we are privileged to have access to the latest medical technology.

The Master—It is useful in the majority of cases, do you not agree?

A Foreigner—Yes it is.

The Master—It means that it frees one from a great ill; it is advantageous to suffer with pain as long as health is recovered.

A Foreigner—Ah! Undoubtedly.

The Master—"Although people that do not think this way, and are attacked by grave ills, they find the contrary medium not to suffer; avoiding the opportune treatment from medics to cure the maladies from their body, or usage of medicine, fearing with the similar behavior of children who are being applied a cure for their ills. Undoubtedly, the root of this conduct lies in their ignorance towards the advantages of health and the good constitution of the body. They see that the treatment is painful, but are blind to its utility. They ignore how lamentable a sick body is. For this motive, they make great strides to escape medication and to not be seen free from the disease"[1] Do we grant this or negate it?

A Foreigner—We will surely grant it.

The Master—"Therefore, it is precise to elevate ourselves over everything, rejecting fear, and to submit with eyes closed and strength. Similarly, to submit to a medic and the treatments, to be consecrated to the continuation of the good and honest, without acknowledging pain"[1] Are you willing to do it?

A Foreigner—I will adjust to whatever comes.

The Master—Tell me now, concisely, what danger or evil threatens to deprive you from reason, since you fear madness so much.

A Foreigner—I will try to describe it to you without hesitation, and I will not omit whatever is necessary with something else of a much better effort. I have told you that I am suffering from depression, and it is understood that it is due to my fear of madness; which can be said in plain words as the terror of losing one's mind. It takes place for no absolute reason, simply when a group of thoughts suddenly overpower me, and they become so persuasive that I end up accepting them. Once convinced, I believe of an inevitably tragic future, with a torment similar to those of the worst mental sufferings rendered by madness; which would be of prolonged and never ending states of derangement and desperation. In the best of cases, death would be the only remedy to escape from my own hell. Who having thought of this as certain, would not be able to feel terror? Comparing my suffering with the various characteristics and varieties of madness, according to medical

---

[1]—Gorgias o de la Retórica (Sócrates VS. Apolo)

classifications, I find that these descriptions correspond to the terms of obsession, probably neurosis and even neurasthenia. Hence in my soul, there is no great concentration of anything harmful, the ideas and preoccupation that govern the mind, and are named: "fixed ideas associated with impulses of irresistible fear". This definition is, a feature of my suffering, and a characteristic of my obsessions; what is obviously an illness, which can additionally drive me completely mad.

The Master—I understand. The similarity between the characteristics of your suffering with those of obsession, neurosis and perhaps neurasthenia, are what makes you firmly believe that you are sick and threatened by madness.

A Foreigner—Exactly.

The Master—In fact, the distinct features of this nature are fixed ideas with impulses of irresistible fear. Is this not right?

A Foreigner—Yes, and it is an ill-fated case for me.

The Master—Do you believe, without similarity to other illnesses, that there exists any particular abnormal sign that we should consider as relevant?

A Foreigner—It could only be by the fixed ideas with impulses of irresistible fear. Regardless, I would like to be sure.

The Master—Likewise, answer what I inquire. How do you understand health?

A Foreigner—Simple, when a human being is in a state where he could normally practice all bodily and spiritually functions, then that human being is healthy. Or, where there is no alteration of health. Ostensibly, since I am sick, I cannot normally practice all my bodily and spiritual functions.

The Master—Bilaterally, if you somewhat fear an illness, it is because you fear an alteration somewhat grave to your body or soul. Is it not infallible?

A Foreigner—Yes.

The Master—And is it not true that to observe and identify any type of health alteration, it is only possible once it can appear and be perceived in determined bodily and soul manifestations?

A Foreigner—I believe so.

The Master—Then, what appears or manifests from your alterations are, only, by the ideas associated with impulses of irresistible fear?

A Foreigner—Yes.

The Master—Jointly, if the fixed ideas associated with impulses of irresistible fear are the only sign of your alteration, does it mean that you only fear this?

A Foreigner—"What else would you like from what you have already strongly verified?"[22]

The Master—From what I have verified? Do you think that it was me that verified it?

A Foreigner—Then who?

The Master—You obviously.

---

[2]—Alcibíades o de la Naturaleza del Hombre (Sócrates VS. Alciabiades)

A Foreigner—Me! At what point!

The Master—"As we start the dialog. Do not become impatient. Look at the tone of this: if I were to ask you, between one and two, which is the bigger number? Wouldn't you respond two?"[2]

A Foreigner—Yes.

The Master—If I were to ask you, how is it bigger?

A Foreigner—By one.

The Master—"Which one of us affirms that two is bigger that one?"[2]

A Foreigner—Me.

The Master—"Is it not me the one that asks the questions and you the one that reponds"[2]

A Foreigner—Yes.

The Master—And about the ideas with irresistible impulses. Is it not me who asked the question and you the one that responded?

A Foreigner—It is correct.

The Master—"And in a conversation of questions and responses, who affirms a statement, the one who asks or the one who responds?

---

[2]—Alcibíades o de la Naturaleza del Hombre (Sócrates VS. Alciabiades)

A Foreigner—The one who responds.

The Master—"And between us, who was the one that affirmed all that we have said?"[2]

A Foreigner—I confess that it is I. Nevertheless, during these moments I cannot agree or disagree. "God willingly nothing will press us, or that it should be of great importance to resume our conversation"[3]

The Master—Do not feel terrified by your usual premature conclusions. We are going to go review once more your words: first, you mentioned that, inadvertently, you feel attacked by strong fears, and then a series of thoughts overcome you. Subsequently, you explain that they enthrall you to the point that you believe that they are certain. It is through this that you see yourself violently tormented. Have I correctly understood you?

A Foreigner—Yes. The more that I believe in them, the more that they press their asphyxiating strength; until my mood is completely out of hope.

The Master—Listen, when some ideas are believed without hesitation, is it because one is persuaded into believing that they true?

A Foreigner—Necessarily.

The Master—What do you think about persuasion? Let us stop for a moment to find this out as if we merely knew about it.

---

[2]—Alcibíades o de la Naturaleza del Hombre (Sócrates VS. Alciabiades)

[3]—Gorgias o de la Retórica (Sócrates VS. Querefón)

A Foreigner—I understand that it is beneficial that I attempt to consolidate this concept as a way to correct any faults that I habitually leave in our path. Well, it is: "to obligate someone to believe or do a certain thing"; it also is: "to provide efficient reasons to mute a ruling or to abandon what followed"; another use is: "to prove something in a particular way, which cannot rationally be negated".

The Master—Would you say that if the thoughts become fixed and associated with impulses of irresistible fear, it is because you find yourself convinced by the work of efficient thoughts that change the ruling.

A Foreigner—It is possible to have it better put.

The Master—Then, they persuade you, given that they are true?

A Foreigner—I repeat, that is what I believe.

The Master—Concerning pain, what allusion should we make in reference to it? It is convenient to talk about this concept, as long as we do not lose cohesion.

A Foreigner—Pain is: "any bothersome and afflictive sensation that one feels in the body, and as far as mood is concerned, it brings forward sentiments of pain and grief."

The Master—From your definition, it is understood that pain is what wounds make the body feel. Likewise, what anxiety, nervousness and fear transmit to the soul.

A Foreigner—Without difficulty.

The Master—Concerning fear or terror, is it something or is it nothing? Take into account that we are trying to go into depth of a capital point. Do not confuse it with the fear that is instantly felt, which is referred to as being scared; this is a fast exciting reflex to a nervous reaction, characterized by being sudden and brief.

A Foreigner—It is specified as: "an anxious perturbation of the mood by harm, or an ill, that threatens or fools the imagination"; it also is: "distrust or apprehension that one has if something contrary to what is wished happens". "With this I understand, that fear is not caused by things that happened nor by those that take place in the present, instead by those that we await; this means that fear is the idea of an ill that we await."[4] Do you approve?

The Master—If from all feared things, it occurs that it deals exclusively with the ills of the future, then it is something that we will not analyze, unless the consequence of our conversation requires it. What is relevant for us is knowing the aforementioned of what fear is: "the anxiety created in the soul by harm or an ill that truly threatens or fools imagination". Or, another way to say this is: "distrust or apprehension that one has if something contrary to what is wished happens." Has it not been loyal to your exposition?

A Foreigner—Dutifully.

The Master—Then, notice, and with great caution tell me: is it possible to live with fear, without thinking in the imminence of an ill or unpleasant idea? Or if you prefer: is it possible to live with this pain, without knowing of any danger or any of the things we reject?

A Foreigner—I think not.

---

[4]—Laques o del Valor (Sócrates VS. Laques y Nicias)

The Master—Will we say that, fear is in part pain and in part thought?

A Foreigner—I accept it.

The Master—Then, these parts are inseparably related or connected?

A Foreigner—How can it be refuted?

The Master—Consequently, fear is fundamentally constituted by pain, in the figure of an anxious perturbation of the soul, and by the real knowledge or imagination of a threat or unpleasant idea; and for its relation and correspondence between them. Have we not grasped its action?

A Foreigner—In what it pertain to me, it is.

The Master—Then, it is appropriate to put in place the final terms for the fixed thoughts, or obsessive, joined to the impulses of irresistible fear. Or will they not be equivalent, the obsessive thoughts, in respect to the knowledge of danger or the unwanted, and the impulses of irresistible fear in respect to distressing pain.

A Foreigner—It seems so.

The Master—And the fixed thoughts, are they joined to the impulses of irresistible fear, with the same conduct, where distressing pain corresponds with the thought that judges and rejects?

A Foreigner—In reality it is essentially the same. I do not see that they can fundamentally differentiate fear, in respect to the obsessive thoughts with irresistible impulses.

The Master—While we both do not find the fundamental difference, we should proceed with the purpose of clarifying the vision of this matter. Let us examine something else. Do not lose track of the principles that I will try to concatenate, luckily they will allow us to find out their nature and what it affects: "when someone does something, is it not necessary that there is a patient that responds to this agent?"[5]

A Foreigner—How is that?

The Master—"What the patient suffers from, is it not identical to the nature of what the agent does? This is what I am trying to say: if someone harms, is it not necessary that something is harmed?"[5]

A Foreigner—Yes.

The Master—"If it is harmed too much, or harmed suddenly, is it not necessary that the thing is harmed in the same format."[5]

A Foreigner—Yes

The Master—"What is harmed, experiences a passion of the same nature as the action of the one that harms."[5]

A Foreigner—Yes.

---

[5]—Gorgias o de la Retórica (Sócrates VS. Polo)

[5]—Gorgias o de la Retórica (Sócrates VS. Polo)

[5]—Gorgias o de la Retórica (Sócrates VS. Polo)

[5]—Gorgias o de la Retórica (Sócrates VS. Polo)

The Master—"In the same way, if someone burns a lot, in a painful way, it is necessary that the thing is burned precisely in the way that is burned"[5]

A Foreigner—I understand.

The Master—"The same happens if something whilst chopped is large, or profound or painful, the chopped thing is exactly the way it was cut."[5]

A Foreigner—Yes.

The Master—"In one word, do you concede value to any other thing from what I just said? The patient suffers from what the agent does, just as it was intended to be produced"[5]

A Foreigner—I concede.

The Master—Now concatenate on this example: if a man shoots an arrow with an arch, our archer would be the agent and the arrow the patient.

A Foreigner—Yes.

The Master—Although, at the moment of impact, something will be hurt, and another one the assailant. The thing that harms is the arrow or the agent, and what is harmed is the victim or the patient.

A Foreigner—Certainly.

---

[5]—Gorgias o de la Retórica (Sócrates VS. Polo)
[5]—Gorgias o de la Retórica (Sócrates VS. Polo)

The Master—At the moment of shooting, the arrow is the patient of the archer, meaning that the arrow is initially an effect of the agent, and moments later, the cause of harm to the patient.

A Foreigner—Sure.

The Master—Then, we will say that the arrow is the effect at the time of the shooting and cause of the wound.

A Foreigner—Yes.

The Master—But, is it possible that the arrow is at one moment the cause and effect over the same thing; cause and effect at the time of shooting, or cause and effect in the wound?

A Foreigner—It is inconceivable.

The Master—Will it be possible that at one point, and over the same thing, for an agent to be the cause and also the effect?

A Foreigner—There is no way.

The Master—Pay attention to what I am about to say. Also, just like a suspicious guardian, do not allow entry to anything bizarre that you distrust. Will you deny that change is to convert one thing into another, or to cede one thing into another?

A Foreigner—There is no reason.

The Master—In that case, we do not ignore that for one thing to become another, the existence is indispensable of the thing that cedes and the one that is ceded. And analogously, it is indispensable that, the agent causing the change, should be different from the thing that is ceded. Is there an absolute fault?

A Foreigner—I do not know if I have understood you correctly. I would must rather prefer that you explanation be less abstract to me.

The Master—Alright, let us assign concrete examples to these words: when the work of an sculptor has transformed the block of marble into a sculptural figure, then the block of marble is the thing that cedes, the sculpture the thing that is ceded, and the sculptor the agent who causes or makes the block change into an sculpture. Is it not simple?

A Foreigner—Yes.

The Master—Therefore, the sculptor is essentially different than the block of marble. Briefly, the agent causing the change is essentially different from the thing that cedes. Is there a doubt?

A Foreigner—None.

The Master—As an analogy: when the juice from grapes is converted into wine, the juice is the thing that cedes, the wine the thing that is ceded, and the ferment, the agent that makes the juice become wine.

A Foreigner—Yes.

The Master—Likewise, the ferment is of a different kind than the juice of the grapes; translating the words into our used language, the causing agent is of a different kind than what is ceded. Is it not true?

A Foreigner—Yes.

The Master—Then, it is possible the the block, the sculpture and the sculpture and the sculptor can be cause and effect at the same time. This can be perfectly extended to the juice, wine and ferment.

A Foreigner—Nothing more certain.

The Master—So, it is indispensable that the block of marble exists before the sculptural figure. Also, that before the wine, the juice of the grape exists.

A Foreigner—Absolutely.

The Master—Consequently to an apple, what would happen to it? Is it not inevitable that before it is ceded, there exists in advance the thing that cedes?

A Foreigner—Yes.

The Master—And that the thing that cedes be essentially different than the agent or than the agents that cause the change?

A Foreigner—Yes.

The Master—And what is your opinion of the rest of the fruits? Is it not necessary that before they are ceded, there exists something that cedes, and that it is essentially different than the agent or the causing agents?

A Foreigner—Who would deny it?

The Master—And in a horse, would we not say that the thing that cedes are the seeds, distinct in their nature to the causing agents?

A Foreigner—Naturally.

The Master—Is there an animal that to be born it could renounce the thing that cedes, or that it can be distinct from its causing agents?

A Foreigner—I do not imagine so.

The Master—Nevertheless, do plants possess the property to renounce the thing that cedes?

A Foreigner—Not even plants.

The Master—And when rain is produced, is it not named condensation when the gaseous state of the vapor of the water is ceded to a liquid state?

A Foreigner—Yes.

The Master—Is it not the same that when rocks are formed, they are ceded by the cooling of a mass of melted minerals. Or that when an aggregation of natural materials in the surface of the earth, cede to consolidate the sediments. Or also, when by the action of the pressure and temperature, the consolidation of the rock cedes a new mineralogical composition?

A Foreigner—Without a problem.

The Master—Would we not also say this about any other phenomenon that takes place?

A Foreigner—I believe that it should be that way.

The Master—Is it now clear? For one thing to become another, it is necessary to first have the ceded thing and then the one that is ceded, where the causing agent, or agents, are different to the thing that they cede.

A Foreigner—Yes.

The Master—Given that you understand, we can deduce that it is impossible for fear to be the cause and effect over itself; furthermore, it cannot do without the thing that it cedes and the composition in which it is constituted. Also, it is not feasible for the causing agent, or agents, to be the same to the thing that they cede.

A Foreigner—No, it is less clear. It disconnects from was said before: that the fixed or obsessive thoughts, or in defect, the impulses of fear, cede to change the reciprocal and immediate relation between these two parts—thoughts as one part, pain with the aspect of impulses of irresistible fear, as the second part.

The Master—While we do not find it, let us leave aside its disposition, and guard the course of our investigation as if it was an invaluable jewel. However, if it becomes inescapable, we should find it. Undoubtedly, the direction that we look at will take us to it, as if it was an alley without an exit. So, concentrate in the thing that it cedes, and imagine if suddenly we would be able to make it disappear, which is comparable to taking the steeds off a cart. Do you wait, even though with singular absence, for the thing that it cedes? That fear will rise without any obstacle?

A Foreigner—No, it is unthinkable. By rejecting the thing that it cedes, the thing that is ceded would not exist. It is completely settled.

The Master—If your vigor would allow it, apply yourself immediately and also imagine that we are able to dismember its parts, or to impede their relation. Then, do you wait for it to not be affected, or that the fear does not disappear?

A Foreigner—Would it then not be what fear is¿

The Master—Overall, we do not ignore that fear cannot exclude the thought that it knows and rejects, nor distressing pain; even though the causing agents of change are obscure to us.

A Foreigner—Let us slow down. Up to this point, I agree that the two parts and indispensable.

The Master—And as the phenomenon of fear starts, or even before, it is precise to believe in the imminence of harm or the undesirable. Without this thought of reject, we understand that there is no space for fear, or for the fixed thoughts with the impulses of irresistible fear.

A Foreigner—No, how¿!

The Master—Also, you have noted that, at the moment of awaking, thoughts overpower you to the point that you have them as certain. By this, you see yourself pressured, by the work of very efficient reasons, to accept its ruling.

A Foreigner—Fatally.

The Master—"If there is someone that whilst conversing with another, pretends to thoroughly understand that which is being said, then be sure that I am fortunate to be one of them. For this reason my friend, I want you to answer to my demand with our own criterion"[6]. "Apply your spirit to the object that occupies us and that only one thing concerns you: the conclusion to our reasoning"[7].

---

[6]—Gorgias o de la Retórica (Sócrates VS. Gorgias)
[7]—Carmides o de la Sabiduaría (Sócrates VS. Critias)

At the beginning of our conversation, you confessed that one particular fear pursued you: the fear of apparitions, which at all cost you wished to avoid. Even though they never appeared in front of you, you were convinced that at any moment they would reveal themselves. You believed of this situation to be a great ill, or as the worsts of the ills. Then, you rectified that only apparitions and voices represented by the imagination could disturb you, as long as they, under extraordinary circumstances, will allow themselves to be seen or heard; with the similarity to the images and sounds sensitive to the senses. In the same form, you would be moved by the images that, by the influx of the world of the dead, would manifest themselves to your eyes and those of humanity. Then, on purpose, you reflected and deterred with the argument that, if you feared them so much, it was because it was very probable or inevitable that you could go insane. Have these not been the thoughts that assault your mind?

A Foreigner—I do not deny it.

The Master—In this new context we reinitiate our voyage, examining the concepts of madness and its disposition, beginning with the principles that we present to our judgment. Of which, in a few words, we call the characteristics or joint of the distinctive signs of the altercations of your soul this: "fixed thoughts associated to the impulses of irresistible fear", not without recognizing that this is the only altercation and motive of care. Tell me, is there something that it is not in its place, or due to carelessness, that we have forgotten?

A Foreigner—There is nothing more complete.

The Master—And, by disposition of its parts, it is necessarily required that a relation or connection exists amongst them; between the obsessive thoughts and the impulses of irresistible fear. Where, obsessive thoughts should be efficiently persuasive, by containing ideas that are unobjectionable or hardly answerable; that at a fixed point is how certain fears are progressively more unbearable. And where, it is impossible that the irresistible fears can do without any of these two parts. Have we not completed it?

A Foreigner—With complete accuracy.

The Master—Because of the reasons we have just discussed, "you should know that I do not know any of the obsessive thoughts that torment you, nor the motive that make them effective or rationally undeniable. It is not because I suspect of what you want to refer to, I will not stop to question how it is that it incites or over what. If I interrogate you instead of communicating my speculations is so our conversation flows in a way that we can clearly know the issue that we are treating. Look now if I have a reason to interrogate you. If I were to ask you: to what style of painting does Zeuxis belong to, and you were to answer that he paints animals, would I not have a motive to ask you what animals does he paint and over what?" [8]

A Foreigner—Of course.

The Master—"To which, are there other painters that paint animals?"[8]

A Foreigner—Surely.

The Master—"If Zeuxis would have been the only one that painted them, then your response would have been correct".

---

[8]—Gorgias o de la Retórica (Sócrates VS. Gorgias)
[8]—Gorgias o de la Retórica (Sócrates VS. Gorgias)

A Foreigner—That is a given.

The Master—"Arithmetic and the arithmetic, do not they teach us what is relative to numbers?" [8]

A Foreigner—Yes.

The Master—"At the same time they persuade us"[8]

A Foreigner—Yes.

The Master—"So, arithmetic equally produces persuasion".[8]

A Foreigner—We cannot refute it.

The Master—"If we were asked: what persuasion and over what? We would say, that which teaches us the quantity of the number, whether it is even or odd. Subsequently, we are in our right to ask, just like we did in respect to the painter, what is the object and, that which it persuades, to what does it refer to?"[8] Is this not an adequate question to be set in place?

A Foreigner—Certainly in a good place.

The Master—"Answer, given that you think the same."[8]

A Foreigner—Me! It is not my intention to misunderstand myself. In reality, I do not know what to say and I feel as if my head is a knot. I am afraid to think that this knot could drive me mad.

---

[8]—Gorgias o de la Retórica (Sócrates VS. Gorgias)

[8]—Gorgias o de la Retórica (Sócrates VS. Gorgias)

[8]—Gorgias o de la Retórica (Sócrates VS. Gorgias)

[8]—Gorgias o de la Retórica (Sócrates VS. Gorgias)

The Master—"Does not the duty of a good hunter consist in never becoming tired or being fooled?"[9]

A Foreigner—Perhaps it could be that no such persuasions exist, and that simply, a hindering comes at certain moments, or a cloud to my mental faculties; without suspecting that I do not accomplish a complete way to develop myself.

The Master—"It seems that you have gotten used to carefully reasoning, but you do not answer that I have asked you"[8]

A Foreigner—Why do you say that?

The Master—Because having asked you about the nature and object of persuasive thoughts, you make mention of a possible cause that you suspect, but you do not speak of those persuasions.

A Foreigner—"I do not dodge it, even if I am not an expert in this type of scrutiny, neither do I fake feeling suffocated by being tangled and not being able to describe what is happening to me. Understand that after having experimented countless times, the passion for strong apprehensions, I cannot achieve to free myself from tremendous confusions, nor adding something that could be slightly useful."

"Contact with you is equivalent to that of a torpedo fish, it paralyzes and confuses; you oblige to look at oneself in an unfamiliar way."[10.]

You should know that the undertaking that I have proposed to you is not an easy subject. Although, in front of your eyes,

---

[9]—Laques o del Valor (Sócrates VS. Laques)

[10]—Menon o de la Virtud (Sócrates VS. Menon

or to anyone's who would want to follow us, nothing is complicated, nor with a motive to disembroil. Nonetheless, to me it is a serious and confusing mess, as if I were in a complex labyrinth where life would be dependent in finding an exit.

The Master—"In the entirety of what I have said, there is no certainty that it is the truth. Then, in my opinion, in the course of every controversy, I have tied and joined the reasons that illustrate that I am not incorrect; and no one that converses with me has been able to sustain an opinion contrary to mine. Hence, I suppose that my opinion is the correct one." [10]

You do not have to reply immediately, if you discern it without benefit. Nonetheless, do not allow yourself to be defeated before the battle has ended. Gather your best weapons, strength and reason, and do not allow yourself to be deterred by a rushed judgment.

A Foreigner—Let us try again, just as we have been doing, leading me with your questions.

The Master—"What other thing can we say? Will we maintain the opinions that we have left planted? Is it not necessary that, what has been affirmed, agrees with what we have planted before?" [11]

A Foreigner—In effect, I understand you, this is why I have not wanted to answer. It is advantageous to have you interrogate me.

The Master—Take a deep breath from the fresh air so that we recapitulate our dialog. Posteriorly you will say: if you presume

---

[10]—Menon o de la Virtud (Sócrates VS. Menon
[11]—Carmides o de la Sabiduría (Sócrates VS. Critias)

that, the cause that incites the impulses of irresistible fear is a hindering in the moments that cloud your mental faculties.

A Foreigner—Possibly.

The Master—But what concept will we establish of the persuasive ideas that efficiently make you fear, are they really not efficient?

A Foreigner—Yes. I sense that at certain moments my judgment becomes cloudy. There are instances in which, suddenly, anything seems to be persuasive, and this is perhaps why at this moment I am apprehensive to comment on it; for being a persuasion dependent of this rarity.

There is where the cause of my illness originates. This illness has stationed itself in my soul, generating a secret and unknown corruption, including being transcendent by being incurable.

The Master—Then, if the obsessive ideas did not turn out to be the product of irrefutable reasoning, would we say that they are inefficient or nothing?

A Foreigner—Perhaps it is inefficient reasoning. I repeat, what mainly worries me is believing that I could become mad, without having anything else than this and its consequences. We have observed that the impulses of irresistible fear are the only symptoms when thoughts overpower me. Mental altercations are nothing else, but the obsession itself, sufficient motive and cause of great excitation, which uncontrollably make me believe in the danger that I am in. It is in the virtue of what we already know, of those thoughts that overpower my soul, through thoughts that become fixed by concern, and continue inevitably next to fierce invincible impulses.

If I understand well, without any objection, so that there exist irresistible fears, the obsessive thoughts should be inseparable to the strong impulses of fear; and it is in total necessity to blindly believe in these thoughts. Since by wanting to exactly know the irrefutable reasons, by which I find myself obliged to firmly believe, I felt dismayed when discovering that such reasons that justify the obsessions do not exist. Immediately, my thoughts became attacked by great fright whilst asking myself if it matters whether or not there are efficient reasons. Evidently, the fixed thoughts do not require from them in order to be dreadfully irresistible. What makes me think in a mental affectation, which is still momentary, is that it could be permanent. By which, my explanation is circumscribed in the frightening news to recognize the power of obsessive ideas; for being diabolically capable of persuading, to the point that they refuse to find refuge in the intelligent reasons. And I doubt at every step, if its power is so great, that it extends to refuse even the inefficient reasons.

The Master—"It happens many times in battle that a life can easily be saved by throwing away ones arms and asking for mercy to the enemy; there many ways to avoid danger when one is in a position to say or do it all." [12] Ah! Friend, do not go through the dishonor that awaits my prosecutors, and firmly submit to what we now face. I tell you, there is nothing more important now for us than to explore that nest of diffused, or disorderly, ideas that so much affliction has given you. Let us find out how they affect you when it is something or when it is nothing.

A Foreigner—There is no greater hope for me to leave this burden that I live, than to follow you to an open path.

---

[12]—Diálogos de Platon, Apología de Socrates (Sócrates VS 556 Jueces)

The Master—Let us begin by remembering what Anaxagoras of Clazomenae enunciated in his theory: "Without intelligence, all things would be mixed and confused, with the minimum inequality amongst them". And he explains that: "the appearance is a simplistic vision of what we see, our first impression, our ordinary senses alone, are too weak to allow us to judge the truth. However, this does not mean that the truth is inaccessible; reflection and experimentation could point to the error and discover order". He adds: "in intelligence, the ordering principle could be found. It penetrates unlimitedly everything that exists, extracting shapes from shapelessness. It could be something that never rests, something that is always active, and something that advances unlimitedly. In all, by not proceeding with it, all distinction would cease to exists, because it is the prelude to the creation of the universe; the force that creates order from disorder, the supreme cause, and the mightiest that we know"[13]. Do you suppose he is mistaken?

A Foreigner—I presume that he has not.

The Master—Intelligence is capable of sustaining and maintaining a man.

A Foreigner—How could it not be? It is certainly what man does.

The Master—And we also do not call it ingenuous, if after thinking up or inventing things, we achieve what is wished and resolve difficulties.

A Foreigner—Of course. It is the conductor and guide in the imagination. It is the author of the survival of man on earth.

---

[13]—Pericles el Ateniense, de Rex Warner, Editorial Hermes

The Master—"Then, do you consider that it is good and useful that intelligence establishes order and repair, so that it reigns in a house or ship?" [14]

A Foreigner—You can be sure I accept it.

The Master—"And using the same words in respect to our body. What do you answer?"[14]

A Foreigner—Yes.

The Master—"In respect to our soul, will it not be if it is integrally established in it order and rule?"[14]

A Foreigner—Yes.

The Master—"It seems to me that giving the tile of healthy entails that intelligence maintains in the body the order, where health is born, and the rest of good corporal qualities". Is it not true?"[14]

A Foreigner—To my understanding, yes.

The Master—"And will it be the legitimate law, if it maintains in order and rule in the soul, which is what moderate and just men conform to; whose effect is justice and temperance?"[14]

A Foreigner—Yes.

---

[14]—Gorgias o de la Retórica (Sócrates VS. Callicles)
[14]—Gorgias o de la Retórica (Sócrates VS. Callicles)
[14]—Gorgias o de la Retórica (Sócrates VS. Callicles)
[14]—Gorgias o de la Retórica (Sócrates VS. Callicles)
[14]—Gorgias o de la Retórica (Sócrates VS. Callicles)

The Master—As long as, during the moments where the ideas are obsessive and are accompanied by the impulses of invisible fear, intelligence becomes obscure, and inevitably order and repair become altered or disturbed.

A Foreigner—I think the same.

The Master—As long as it remains in this mode, it will be very difficult for you to highlight the qualities and relations of the nature of things. Then, starting with the occurrences of some event, the reasons and concepts will not be able to be chained to natural and legitimate inferences that justify what has just happened, nor will they be able to adduce in support to any demonstration. In sum, all things will remain confused and mixed.

From there, without being effectively persuasive, any idea seduces you. Is this not your luck?

A Foreigner—Emphatically yes.

The Master—Like this, in conditions of chaos and disintegration, your reasoning demonstrates incongruence; with the unconcealed consequence that whilst developing a thought, it is embarrassing to head towards an objective, and to remain in this topic or in any other you wish to choose.

A Foreigner—Do not feel obligated to repeat it. I concede entirely.

The Master—I do not accustom to leave my obligations in the hands of sensations; as if before taking into account the importance of every step we take, I would be cautious of not tiring or making you uncomfortable.

Therefore, let us return to the issue. "I suspected that your anomalies would derive from this proceeding. However, I have not wanted to say anything, so that you do not become surprised if, in the course of the discussion, I bring forward things that seem evident. It is not so I appear to be biased, but for the conversation to flow with finality, and that we do not acquire the habit of preventing and guessing our thoughts by vain conjectures." [15]

If you are not satisfied, let us both go forward and examine the case where certain ideas in the sane man interact.

There is one thing that appears in our mind, and it is image. Here, colors, shapes and sizes of the material world are stored. They are introduced by the sense of sight, and they are assimilated by the attributes of the human being.

A Foreigner—Yes.

The Master—Because of this, we have concrete and particular images over a determined object.

A Foreigner—Continue.

The Master—On the other hand, it is logic that names the intellectual representation of the image an idea or concept. Given this example, we know that there are ships of several sizes and figures. This is due by the ingenuity of the builder, who builds according to the service that it wishes to provide to each one; therefore, there exist triremes used for war. Some are long, so it can transport soldiers, but there light ones, and also the Phoenician galleries which are also used for war. However they are dissimilar in the space distribution of their paddles. Is this not a fact?

---

[15]—Diálogos de Platon, Gorgias o de la Retórica (Sócrates VS. Callicles)

A Foreigner—Without a doubt.

The Master—Regardless, the concept of a boat is only one: a floating object which is more or less concave, which is used for transportation on water.

A Foreigner—I understand the features of each one.

The Master—The same can be said about chairs, whose concept is being a piece of furniture used for seating.

A Foreigner—Yes.

The Master—With the antecedent, it is now clear that in the mind there are images and concepts, which are both different in substance.

A Foreigner—It seems correct. Continue.

The Master—Let us call these simple concepts, ideas where nothing is affirmed or denied, they are neutral and barely refer to the existence of the objects. For example, words such as: love, truth, man, hose, book, whiteness, and beauty; which can normally be expressed with one sole word, unless it is not an obstacle to express them in two or more words. Notice: "the green leaves of summer". Have you understood me?

A Foreigner—Without a problem.

The Master—Lastly, we will say of these ideas that they cannot be imagined; they lack color, size and figure. Amongst them all, perhaps we will not find any more elemental than the word omen, being, thing or God. Subsequently, they can be represented with one or many words. Consequently, it does not possess a persuasive effect in the mind. Or are we mistaken?

A Foreigner—This precedent cannot be denied.

The Master—We have come this far, and if we recognize the validity of what the judgment says, it can be deduced that it is: "The affirmation of the relation between two ideas". Or, without going too far from your lexicon: "the expression that affirms or denies something". This involves a complete thought. Let us exemplify: "the man is seated in the bench, the leaves are green". To judge is the same as affirming or denying something. In sum, it is a group of related ideas that affirm or deny the existence of a certain thing.

A Foreigner—Yes, we recognize it.

The Master—Let us leave the study of logic for a better occasion. Let us accept or deny whatever you have to say about reasoning.

A Foreigner—Let it be what you say. It is argued that reasoning is the participation of various joined judgments with a determined order; which we have been discussing.

The Master—If you can distinguish between the idea of the judgment and concept, let us return to the point that we left inconclusive. Tell me, what would happen with the judgments that are persuasively efficient, when the relation between the group of ideas is not clear?

A Foreigner—That linked in a vague way, they would necessarily have a confusing meaning.

The Master—Then, the judgments or arguments that derive from here, will be inadmissible or undetermined?

A Foreigner—One would hope.

The Master—Finally, will a sensible man believe in such ideas? Or will he be persuaded by absurd judgments, accompanied by unbearable agitations of horror. Will it be factual that this will happen to him?

A Foreigner—It is inconceivable.

The Master—Even with the previous concept, do you believe that the fixed or obsessive ideas that are associated with the impulses of invincible fear do not contain arguments or efficient reasons? And perhaps, inefficient to persuade; in sum, besides being vague ideas, they turn out to be very suggestive.

A Foreigner—What more.

The Master—And if you firmly believe in absurd and incoherent ideas, it has been because of temporal affections that, to a certain degree, make your mental faculties disorderly; given the sudden disorder, during which the ideas are obsessive and very dominant.

A Foreigner—I will say yes.

The Master—Given that, in this situation, it is ineludible to believe in the eminence of an ill; as if it was maintained with irrefutable arguments. And the more that you create in those ideas, the more frightening they will be. Is this not what is happening?

A Foreigner—You have accurately illustrated my illness.

The Master—Now, let us reflect with a fresh approach: Have you ever seen before fully sane men who, regardless, fear many things?

A Foreigner—Yes I have seen them. However, there is no point of comparison with me, because they do not fear as much, or for such absurd things.

The Master—By all the Gods! Not so absurd!

A Foreigner—That is what I have said!

The Master—After such a long road, we are back here again.

A Foreigner—What do you refer to exactly?

The Master—Simply follow along. I beg you to pay attention. Hopefully we do not unintentionally begin to converse in frivolous way. The fixed ideas associated to the irresistible impulses are: confusing ideas that momentarily seem to be persuasive, but that during the moments when they are free of disturbance, they cannot continue to be fearfully persuasive; albeit, outside of these destitute moments, the mental operations of your soul fully accomplish their functions; in an intelligence that provides the capacity to exercise its function. However, you live frightened to not go mad, since outside the moments of obnubilation, you are fully capable to discern certain things; or as you mentioned, discerning "such absurd things", which is not devoid of reason. It is precisely this fact that makes the causes that attrivute to your disease doubtful. Can you explain to me, how is it that you are so terrified towards madness, or better yet, to the absurd ideas being in such a lucid state without suspecting it? Or, how have you not been concerned to discover why? If you are not able to formulate it with simplicity, then try to present it again. Do not feel discouraged if you have to repeat it, we will do it as many times as it is needed. Remember that the best pieces of china are not done by the apprentice.

A Foreigner—Do not hope that it is I who will procure to clear up such a mess. So, if you cannot clear up what you see as contradictory, we will have to wait until, before we present any points, I become tangled without escape; especially since these issues are not only terrorizing, but completely frighten me when I attempt to face them.

The Master—Take a deep breath, and do what the Spartan soldiers did before battle: "feel as if you possess nothing more than a soul and will". Be conscious that your only obligations are to accomplish your tasks to the best that you can. Even if you are not victorious, your best consolation will be realizing that you did what was correct. Be generous and grant yourself a truce, as long as it does not reserve any thought that contributes conciseness.

A Foreigner—Thank you for being so patient with me, since all you have in front of you is a man besieged by the enemy.

The Master—"It is important for important things to be said two or three times" [16]. Let us see if we are fortunate, and reaffirm what we know: fear is partly a thought that senses threat and a sentiment of anxiety. Both are different, but are ligated with one purpose.

A Foreigner—I know!

The Master—It is impossible for fear to disregard any of its parts.

A Foreigner—Yes.

The Master—Then, it lacks the thought that judges and rejects.

---

[16]—Gorgias o de la Retórica (Sócrates VS. Callicles)

A Foreigner—Yes.

The Master—And, in the way that you have it as certain: it firmly obsesses.

A Foreigner—I also concur.

The Master—And our thought can create a real risk or one that is purely imaginary.

A Foreigner—Yes.

The Master—Naturally, the sane man believes imaginary things, however, he will not accept ideas that are ostensibly absurd or incoherent.

A Foreigner—I agree. Believe me, after such excitement in your part, it would be embarrassing not to make a great effort to continue.

The Master—If you have spoken from your heart, let us continue again. Take a deep breath and make my question your objective. Give me at least a general idea. How is it that obsessive ideas are infallibly persuasive?

A Foreigner—By God! If have abstained from attempting to describe them is simply by the fact that I have not identified coherent reasons after several attempts. They are in the middle of a series of ideas, which are arguments that attempt to persuade, as well as ideas that are intensely persuasive. These same ideas are now fundamental and a term in an argument. The fear to cease is connected with me, just like that of the fish and the water. By which, I believe that my only concern is the blind belief of going mad and its incessant and inevitable conclusions, without any other thoughts than the same idea of madness, and those that by this fatality fill uncontrollably my imagination. So, if these same ideas are arguments and terms, I do not find any sense in interpreting them, nor to clearly explain the thoughts that bind me, but that efficiently convince me.

The Master—It is nothing less than a good start, and do not suppose that you have not benefitted from it. It is evident, and you do not ignore it, that I will not cease to ask you questions as many times as our dialog requires. Do not allow for any distractions to come and occupy yourself only with this issue: your fear is the immediate relation between distressing impulses and fixed or obsessive ideas, through a tight stretch. The obsessive ideas are very persuasive, so persuasive in fact, that it is not possible to free yourself from them. With the exception of not being believable in conditions that are mentally normal, by being disconcerting thoughts; by not going through a judgment, they become proposition and conclusion in an argument. If you agree, let us move forward, or let us return to wherever your opinions have moved.

A Foreigner—You should believe that I have not skimped my effort. I cannot decipher why the idea of going mad, along with other ideas, is sufficiently strong to seduce me; so much so, that it is very difficult for to me determine how they begin or end. Rising over everything, and I repeat that I will make an effort to clear this issue, not without warning you that I am not sure if it is surely this way. Let us take a point of departure in which we will suppose that I am invaded by fear; withstanding intensely distressing pain, caused by eminent danger of an ill that I do not categorically want. In this state, there is in me a relation between pain and the knowledge of a threat. Is this not what survives?

The Master—It is what you have recounted.

A Foreigner—In such situation, I do not see greater threat than the idea of going mad, since I feel this way. Then, since said idea becomes a threat, it becomes persuasive. And I do not find any words that make us not go in circles, to whilst attempting to sensibly explain this problem.

The Master—No, it is in the least absurd!

A Foreigner—Do you not understand! They are effective in persuading me. And I am not denying what we have agreed up to this point.

The Master—I say no! Unless you obligate me to accept it by force, I concede.

A Foreigner—"You should know that it is not easy to be near you and avoid a response. You do not leave alone those who come near you, and you force them to verbally fight with you." [17]

I will present this. The threat is the idea of going mad, and it is supported by the firm belief that it is not possible to avoid suffering from this illness, and I ask myself: how can I avoid the eminent danger, if I know that to be afflicted by fear, it is necessary to be persuaded by a threat. The threat that torments me is the idea of the eminent danger of going mad; then, this idea is dangerously planted, since I truly fear going mad, and I know that going insane means to suffer from great torments, which are produced by fear itself. Lastly, I ultimately accept that I will be infinitely ill-fated with madness. That is how it is, I do not ignore that if I fear going mad it is because I dread fear. Also, I do not doubt for an instant that it has been an entanglement of incoherent ideas. It saddens me much more to think that this motive can hinder or ruin our dialog. I even fear that without your help, it would be impossible to stop

---

[17]—Teetetes o de la Ciencia

the disruption that these ideas cause; which seem to me to be a horrible self-destructive circle. Subsequently, without remedy and consumed by my implorations for help, I would certainly accept what disproportionately perturbs me: the most terrifying ideas that my mind can create. Let me tell you, I have begun to tolerate at times, whether asleep or awake, the indescribable fear caused by believing that I can eternally be in a reduced space where it is not even possible to move my body in a comfortable position; similar to a human body buried in a coffin, or trapped in rocks; in a world where it is completely feasible to live like this forever, which is obscure without comparison, without a God, and without a time that will allow me to remember my beginnings or imagine the end; like a mere product of chance that lacks any meaning. If you could believe it, for a few seconds, you would know the horror that I have experienced. It is precisely from this fear that I ask God to protect me. Now, as hard as it can be for me, it is a passing thought; by not being associated to any near threat. Let us not stop here as long as it is ephemeral; which in concretion is similar more to an intense transitory experience by asphyxiation, than to an enigma or question that poses a threat. Especially when I evoke the advice that you gave to Axioco in his death bed: "You are a toy of a new mistake, your fear of death stems from there; you fear seeing yourself without a soul, and you attribute a soul to privation; you are afraid of being insensible, and you imagine a sensibility that makes you take notice of your insensibility". With this point, let us move forward and conclude that if I fear madness it is because I dread the fear that it brings to me; if I dread fear, it is because it is a strong enough of a motive to firmly believe that it would be inevitable to dread fear; and if I do not succeed in dominating the distressing impulses, desperation would augment uncontrollably, which would make m fall in an unstoppable disorder of extremely tormenting ideas. Judge it for yourself!

The Master—It is not more difficult to cook a stone than for you to speak explicitly. Wait, as much as the road overwhelms you, follow me to escape this flood.

From everything that I have presented, I do not believe that we have discussed anything that is troublesome over the object of our conversation, if you yourself have not given testimony over the truth of what I say. And from your part, you have not advanced at all if I do not testify in your favor.

A Foreigner—I know.

The Master—To mimic your language, you are assured that there is no greater concern than the fear from the threat of madness; that you fear madness because, whilst insane, you will inevitably suffer from intolerable torments produced by madness. That it is impossible to restrain the impulses of fear that torment you now, and that if you do not stop them, you will go mad with indescribable suffering as a result of the wild tormenting ideas; without great limit than the amplitude of imagination; comparable to the most vicious vengeance from an enemy.

A Foreigner—It is no less.

The Master—"Be ready my friend, that I will strengthen you with my questions to slowly examine your own judgement." [18]

A Foreigner—Of course. And I want you to know that I feel fortunate that you find interest in my problems.

---

[18]—Carmides o de la Sabiduría o Templanza (Sócrates VS. Critias)

The Master—Notice that you insist on planting ideas that are totally irrational. Consider applying it to other objects and I am sure that it will seem perfectly irrational.

"Do you conceive a view that does not see any of the other things that the other views see, but that it is the view of itself and of other views, and even of what is not seen? Do you conceive a view that does not see color, even though it is a view, even though it sees itself and other views? Do you believe that such a view exists?" [18]

A Foreigner—No.

The Master—"Do you conceive an ear that does not hear any voice, and suddenly it heard itself and other ears, and even what is not an ear?" [18]

A Foreigner—Neither that.

The Master—"Considering all the senses at once, is it possible for one to be the sense of itself and other senses, but it does not feel anything that the other senses do?" [18]

A Foreigner—Certainly no.

The Master—"Or that there is a wish that is not the wish of pleasure, that it only is for itself and other wishes?" [1]

A Foreigner—No.

---

[18]—Carmides o de la Sabiduría o Templanza (Sócrates VS. Critias)
[18]—Carmides o de la Sabiduría o Templanza (Sócrates VS. Critias)
[18]—Carmides o de la Sabiduría o Templanza (Sócrates VS. Critias)
[1]—Diálogos de Platón, Apología de Sócrates (Sócrates VS 556 Jueces)

The Master—"A will that does not want any good, and that it will commonly like itself and other wills?" [18]

A Foreigner—No.

The Master—"Can you conceive that there exists love, that it is not love of any gender of beauty, instead of itself and of the other loves?"[18]

A Foreigner—No.

The Master—"Can you imagine an opinion that is not the opinion of itself or of the other opinions, and it does not refer to any of the ordinary object of the opinion?"[18]

A Foreigner—No.

The Master—"Can you imagine a science that is not the science of any particular knowledge, instead of itself and the sciences that it differs from?"[18]

A Foreigner—I imagine no.

The Master—And having accessed each one of my petitions, do you affirm that a fear exists that fears itself and the rest of the fears, but it does not fear any danger or malaise?

A Foreigner—I know that I am before ambivalence. Regardless, it seems as though fear would have the strength to originate by itself, or if it needed something, it would know to provide

---

[18]—Carmides o de la Sabiduría o Templanza (Sócrates VS. Critias)
[18]—Carmides o de la Sabiduría o Templanza (Sócrates VS. Critias)
[18]—Carmides o de la Sabiduría o Templanza (Sócrates VS. Critias)
[18]—Carmides o de la Sabiduría o Templanza (Sócrates VS. Critias)

itself somehow. I know it is absurd, but it persuades me with no repair, without clearly achieving the lack of congruence to finally stop believing in them. Similarly, one sole voice becomes many with an echo, the idea of fear turns into many, becoming preponderantly suggestive with itself.

The Master—"Are you speaking to yourself, or is it an answer, or are you presenting an issue? I certainly do not understand you" [19]

A Foreigner—I have answered you. Better yet if you chose to receive the question.

The Master—Congratulations! "Which one of the two do you want us to discuss first? Notice that the two are disparate." [19] First: If the thought that contains such group of ideas is capable to persuading itself. Second: of the ability it has to provide itself from some or various thoughts.

A Foreigner—Since you have made it perceptible, decide which one better suits you.

The Master—Let us reflect on whatever happens, when the aforementioned group is enough to make itself irresistible. We said that if simple concepts relate in a vague form, we will unforgivingly observe a confusing argument. Do you remember?

A Foreigner—Of course.

The Master—And is it not in my opinion referenced to: if they are unappreciated, by being vague and confusing, will it be

[19]—Gorgias o de la Retórica (Sócrates VS. Polo)
[19]—Gorgias o de la Retórica (Sócrates VS. Polo)

that the relation that exists between said concept is neither natural nor legitimate?

A Foreigner—Will this disembroil?

The Master—When the concepts or ideas occur amongst each other, they do not do it with the order that follows nature or reason; where such order goes through obligatory conditions, or exclusively in necessary obligatory conditions that derive from nature. Whilst occurring, they do not subject themselves to any rule or law; as if we sustained that "all animals are born white". In this example, I propose a group of ideas where they group themselves just as they appear. Nevertheless, the relation that exists amongst them is not consistent with the natural; given that, rationally, there is no connection between "all the animals", and the fact of being "born white". Do you agree?

A Foreigner—Yes, it opposes a natural condition.

The Master—Or is it congruent to tell you that not all animal bodies are mortal?

A Foreigner—No, by God.

The Master—Or that all men are just, and subsequently affirm that the no man is just.

A Foreigner—Neither that.

The Master—Or to assure yourself that all numbers are pairs.

A Foreigner—It would not be legitimate.

The Master—Now young friend, does it not coincide with that group of ideas that influence you so much? Since they are rationally incoherent?

A Foreigner—It seems so.

The Master—So, they do not reconcile to the obligatory conditions that follow nature and reason.

A Foreigner—Seemingly, no.

The Master—Then, do you believe them, or do they efficiently persuade you?

A Foreigner—Not exactly.

The Master—Perhaps it is that they spontaneously, and without much intervention of thought, order themselves to be ostensibly credible.

A Foreigner—How can they exhibit themselves that way? Even if they could do it by their own impulse, it would be absurd for them to go in any direction alone.

The Master—Perhaps, in a mental act that you do not recall, this group of ideas disappeared and ideas that efficiently persuasive appeared; as if it dealt with a fault in the memory where they surge in a new and natural arrangement in place of the others; going over all lucubration of thought, with the velocity of a lightening volt that leaps out of a cloud.

A Foreigner—No, this is really not your approach.

The Master—"If you believe that I hold as true what you do not believe is, interrupt and disprove me. I do not speak as a man that is sure of what he is saying, but I am searching with you the truth. So, I do appreciate if you disprove me. If you are correct, I swear that I would agree with you." [20]

Based on this, I will continue digging into this subject: Fear, we ignore that cause, or primary causes, that originate it. It probably obeys to more subtleness of the soul, and it is part of the sublime complexity of humanity, which we are trying to explore. This impedes me from knowing that fear absolutely lacks the thought that judges and rejects harm and danger.

A Foreigner—I presume that in a not so distant future, the mystery that is obscure now can be cleared with further detail.

The Master—Fortunately, it is not difficult to wait for it to happen. Beforehand, answer concretely my question: how has it been possible to believe the absurd ideas to dread fears? Because of this, it will be inevitable to definitely lose the judgment; when at a certain time you recognize the impossibility that any other foolish ideas have in persuading you.

A Foreigner—It is not that. It often strikes me, by a sudden motive that I cannot foresee, that the impulses of grouped fears with frightening ideas surge, which if we carefully analyze, appear to be absurd. By not carefully examining them, they quickly become convincing circumstances that with, my own flesh, I have lived in repeated occasions. This experience has allowed me to confirm that it precise not to escape frightening ideas, nor to defy them; simply, to allow them to be in a position where I could observe them with complete patience; this allows me to judge them as any irrelevant thoughts, or as merely incoherent ideas. Then, the impulses of fear disappear, and I momentarily feel a master of the domain of my passions; believing to be the winner of a

---

[20]—Gorgias o de la Retórica (Sócrates VS. Callicles y Gorgias)

bloody battle. Similar to the great generals who are fooled by the enemy's strategy, proceed with the illusion of victory, but then fall in their fatal trap; given that after a period of relative calm, the impulses of grouped fear manifest themselves again without any warning. Then, I feel obliged to carefully examine them, although I ultimately discover they are harmless. Imagine this story to be multiplied an infinite amount of times; by the reasons I have discussed, it is as if it is a battle without barracks. I continually ask myself: "Will it be useful for me to carry out intelligent thoughts, with great efforts to overcome these fears?" It is just like the work of a charioteer who is forced to guide the ardent horses, going in multiple circles in a cruel path, until one of the horses trips or is weakened in the knees.

The Master—If you assure yourself that the absurd ideas are not persuasive, let us proceed with the second question: You mentioned the ability when the obsessive ideas supply themselves from other thoughts; which are unpredictable, sudden and purely absurd, even uncontainable. Is this not what you have affirmed?

A Foreigner—Yes, I said it. My intention is not to avoid the point, but to breathe with relief.

The Master—If you are not going to help yourself now, do not advance or feel demoralized, that the veil that blinds us will not allow us to move on if you do not search for it with a clear head and serene heart.

As to what concerns me, I do not plan to escape from the prison, nor by the insistences of my friend, unless the inner voice of my demon communicates it to me *.

---

*—In antiquity, a "demon" referred to the divinity attached to the destiny of a person or city. Persuaded that it had been assigned

A Foreigner—I beg that you do not take into account the order of what I am attempting to describe to you. Understand that I do not have the luxury of those who have the authority to hold forth. I am sure that these obsessive ideas are absurd to those who are willing to listen; how would the act of thinking without justification or reason be, with eyes closed, that I am destined for the terrible; that I will inevitably go mad, or that I will never gain control over my fears. If it is not anywhere else, it is because there is no support to have them as certain; regardless, I believe in them momentarily. Here, my major preoccupation is to see them grow incessantly, compared to a tireless fountain; condemned to remain vigilant day and night, until I outdo the limit of my tolerance. I figure that these insulting ideas are carnivorous rats that quickly climb up my body, and as hard as I try, more climb than those that fall.

The Master—What you really fear is not being capable of stopping the absurd and obsessive ideas; since you think that it truly deals with an inexhaustible fountain of frightening ideas.

A Foreigner—That is what I have to discern.

The Master—It follows that: the absurd ideas provide or support themselves in these last ones. In brief, they support themselves through the belief of the impossibility of controlling them, and they reverently become conjunctly fearful. Or, in a different focus, these last ideas have known how to provide themselves from absurd thoughts to persuade together.

---

a special religious mission, whose accomplishment received orders from a divine voice, from a familiar demon.

A Foreigner—I understand! It is those foolish ideas that provide themselves from other thoughts, given that, by themselves, they do not say or do anything.

The Master—Now, tell me more in this respect that I too want to carefully find out. What do you mean when you find yourself required to have intelligent thoughts through great efforts; or to carefully examine the fearful ideas, so we can identify them as: "singularly absurd". By fortune of great labor, do you discover what is unintelligibly absurd?

A Foreigner—By God, no!

The Master—Young friend, you know that there is no exception that obliges us to immediately answer our questions. If you believe that you have nothing to offer, then we will finish today. Tomorrow, when your mood renewed, we will continue; however, if you prefer, you can briefly rest as long as you continue with the guidelines that our dialog demands; with the conciseness and alternation that our questions and answers demand.

A Foreigner—No, no. Do not stop because of me, since the question that you have posed has me very intrigued and I am anxious to continue.

The Master—It is your decision, I am listening.

A Foreigner—As big as my determination can be, I am in darkness, with my intellect frozen, and I convince myself with: what task is this? No, there is no such thing, as long as they are truly absurd and they present themselves in this mode. But what do I say! In sum, what I have said is the pure truth, as if a new known novelty emerged. It is disconcerting to admit that: "to constantly dwell in the irrational, does not represent fatigue or mere effort". And you undeniably have made me express what is exact, it is a concealed consequence to infer that by such efforts not existing, then such threats could not either. It is not difficult to speculate from the past that my greatest ills have been sustained in the subtleness of believing that fear can take place before a threat exists. This implies that the alteration of this delicate order is the fundamental start of my terrible anxiety; which in one word has been: believing that it is reachable, fear the suffering of fear.

Before searching for a way to give a clear meaning to the conclusions, it comes to mind what Anaxagoras of Clazomenae discovered and referred to with great detail in his writings. These thoughts have been exhibited in various forums, which I interpret with the confidence of having understood them adequately. "Appearance is a simplistic vision from which we cannot see our first impression, our sole ordinary senses are too weak to allow us to judge the truth, however, it does not mean that the truth is inaccessible; the reflection and the experimentation can point out errors and discover order" [21] I do not think he was mistaken in this respect, since at some point in his life he also suffered from an interlude of mental disorder; in a state of sordid desperation he knew how to rise. I find that, according to his writings: "none of the strange factors that contributed to the adoption of insane resolutions were important; that only the disorganization of their nature propelled them, against their judgment, to exaggerate them beyond measure" [22].

If what Anaxagoras affirms as certain and we have deceived him by unexpectedly coming to the same points and redound to the same conclusions, we know that by finding errors we would discover the order of things; albeit, by discovering the

---

[21]—Pericles el Ateniense, de Rex Warner
[22]—Gorgias o de la Retórica (Sócrates VS. Callicles)

order of things, we would know the existing error. Do you not approve?

The Master—Do not ask me. It is better if you analyze it, because "the only guarantee that I have so I am not mistaken in discussions, I repeat, is from those I have debated with and have not proved me the contrary". Much like Anaxagoras, or any others, who has said the truth, whilst there is no one more vigorous who can put down his conceptions and demonstrate that he lied.

CHAPTER III

Social Phobia

A Foreigner—Similar to a torch that lights the absolute darkness of a deep and winding cave, thanks to you I have penetrated what I call: the home of fear, the place where it is necessary to be mad or be reckless in order to enter alone. I am surprised at the glimpse of the road we are on with you as a guide.

Whoever knows the origin of your ills is in a position to avoid them, and I have not been the exception; I know with clarity, more than ever, of what primarily attacks me. What is more, that by commending myself to God, I have gained the will to not abandon the fight. Your help is still very vital to me, since I still do not feel free from my obsessions. Not even after learning how to deal with my frightening fear do I excel in understanding what harasses me. This situation I will try to explain to you, despite my language: as if dealt with a heavy bodily burden, which is difficult to let loose; similar to a heavy iron ball that I forcibly drag wherever I go, because the strength needed to break its chains have tied me to it, and it is far superior than my greatest effort. This has been for a very long time the precursor of my sorrows, beginning of my greatest concern, my bitter and veteran enemy: shame, shyness, the fear to blush in front of anyone. If it is difficult for me to speak with sincerity, it is simply because I am prone to embarrassment and this an intense motive of unrest. Whether it is in front of one person, or in front of many, I want to run and hide, since I am incapable of unwinding and being myself. I cannot stand to be embarrassed or paralyzed in front of people, much less in front of those who are strangers, whom I would much less want to discover my defects. I am haunted at the thought that I blush over nothing, or something, whether it is a little or a lot, which to my dismay always manifests in my face with such an evident particularity that I cannot pass as unnoticed. With this complexion, people inevitably look at me with an air that reflects traits or bewilderment or curiosity, even the affliction that they share with me; it seems as if I infected them with a swift and malignant agent. The effect gives me an enormous sentiment of guilt and repudiation towards myself. In all, it is the sum of the scene of my perturbations. Who in this situation will see me as an abnormal man? I would be the fetid man among people who is better to keep away. How will I be able to carry out my tasks? No one would want to have me as a friend, or boyfriend, or husband. I would only be seen with compassion or as a joke, and to my family, with worry and deception. I know that I will ruin happiness with such constant harassment from fear. I cry out for help! Show me the way!

The Master—In such case, it is fundamental to present the battle in order to recuperate the spirit of that thought, which is attempting to affirm something from nothing.

Well, answer: do you agree that, "fear is always a friend of shame and not the other way around; deriving that shame is a variant of fear". If this works as an illustration, follow this model: "an odd number is a variant of a number. Is it not indispensable that in the number the odd number exists? But anywhere the odd number exists there is a number"[1]. Is this not similar to the relation between shame and fear?

A Foreigner—It is clear. "Fear has more reach than fear".

The Master—It is conceived between the two that if fear exists, then the belief is entirely inevitable of a threat, or at least the rejection of an idea or situation which is unwanted.

A Foreigner—We have answered it countless times and I am still in the same position.

---

[1]—Eutifrón o de la Santidad (Sócrates VS. Eutifrón)

The Master—I warn you that I will not be able to exceed what you have proposed, if before thinking of my answer you previse. Let us find the object of our dialog and exclusively comply with what I formulate.

Then, in shame, there exists a inseparable thought in an imminent ill, or in ideas or situations that are rejected.

A Foreigner—The same as in fear.

The Master—Despite the aforementioned, you confess that silently you preserve a pernicious fear, which is shame and shyness. In other words, fear is a variant of itself, or in brief, you fear the embarrassment of shyness.

A Foreigner—Not exactly. I do not pretend to repeat the subject of the suffering of fear; it is something which we have left behind when we agreed that it is something truly incoherent. I am referring to people accusing my fear, of any medium, given that rarities, and bizarre ways, that unexpectedly sprout without being able of being avoided. Thus, it is inevitable for people to observe me; enough of a reason to remain embarrassed and in a state of constriction. I have shown this to you, it is the fear to display my fears, which grow when they present themselves more notorious and unfounded.

The Master—I do not accustom to abandon the reasons that appear just, and you completely understand that nothing that we have left behind is unquestionable; beforehand, let us reconsider, or answer my question so that we can jointly crumble the controversy.

You refer that the authentic motive of your constriction is: that they know or discover you to be a man who is embarrassed or fearful?

A Foreigner—Yes. It embarrasses me to be seen in such a clear way, in front of people, with my mood constricted. Additionally, by thinking that a scene like this will occur, or simply remembering those that were embarrassing; I am so susceptive to this, not only by recalling suffocating situations, but also by discussing them.

The Master—It will be easier for you to see that I am not driven by compassion, rather by the love of the truth.

Subsequently, you do not deserve the least distrust by saying that I have finally understood you, and I allege that it embarrasses you that people are empowered to perceive you this way; whether it is together or separate through the aid of sight, hearing, touch, taste or smell. How can you be understood, given that without any help of the senses there is no mechanism that helps perceive tangible things?

A Foreigner—Do not think that I laughing at you. You have made me look as if I did not add an accent mark by procuring to attribute the act of perception as the root of my constriction. No, what I have wanted to expand with detail are the ills and harms that I provoke to other people with my particularities and bizarreness.

The Master—Try it again!

A Foreigner—Let me begin by telling you that: the concept that is created about a strange man, who with absurd and insane behavior, does not inspire confidence or tranquility; who without the dominion of judgment is incapable of suppressing such unpleasant attitudes, that it becomes bothersome or even offensive to others. All of this configures an idea that deeply saddens me, and that I ceaselessly recall against my will; as if it dealt with uncomfortable guilt, or a important fault that indelibly marks you.

The Master—By Heracles! You do not notice your inadmissibility with what I ask.

A Foreigner—You disorient me!

The Master—I understand that you consider an ill or harm, extravagance, trouble, offenses, your fears, and whatever is unbearable, much like Prometheus' punishment was for stealing the divine fire. But please! Do not speak to me as if they alone are a threat or unbearable, or "as if it exclusively was going to sustain that they are unbearable ideas, which I should recognize in this way, just like the act that you mention"[3]; "since it is far from being clarified, you speak about it as if by pronouncing the word 'rarity' was the same as pronouncing 'embarrassment', or as if 'particularities' was the same as pronouncing 'ills'". It means that to understand it in this acceptation, it is obligatory that they are analogous to the nature of embarrassment, or ills, or the conditions of unbearable ideas.

A Foreigner—I certainly know that it is not the lack of memory that wraps my spirit, rather disorder to level thought.

I have been warned that "speaking with you, leads to plunging into doubt, that you do not know much more than simply doubt"[2], and to my misfortune, I am again immersed in a series of ideas that if I accept as different, I cannot discern with enough clarity.

The Master—"If I bring doubt to the spirit of others, it is not because I know more, on the contrary, I doubt more than anyone, and in this path I make other doubt more." So, "let

---

[3]—Menón o de la Virtud (Sócrates VS. Menón)
[2]—Sofista o del Ser.

us search for such explanations and dissuade whilst thinking that I shall broaden you with my usual questions"[3].

At this point, I do not know what the objects of embarrassment are, or ills, or danger, or unpleasant ideas. However, do not give up against an enemy that does not allow itself to be seen, and pretend with astuteness to dissuade front facing it.

A Foreigner—As much as I ponder, I do not know how to get around it. I am trapped in a jam. Regardless of the inconveniences, you can see it as if dealt with a captain who is sure that his hoplites will abandon their post. I can scarcely add that a man, who does not have the least consideration toward himself, has no reason for living. Obstinately, I sorrowfully say: what future can a man wait for, other than seeing himself rejected; rejected as someone who has contracted the disease; to see what remains of life, the discomfort in the face of those who have the misfortune to deal with me. What do you think is their opinion, just as I am in front of you, when they see me sweating and senselessly blushing? Do you truly believe that anyone in my place can think of a future where he has no opportunity to be wrought? With an existence freed from one sorrow, simply to enter into another.

The Master—I understand. How can you not feel sorry for yourself by sweating and blushing?! Would it not be better if you avoided steam baths, or to leave your house during hot days, or to take long walk without anyone observing you, and to lock yourself in your house to practice the exercises you do in the gymnasium? However, be careful not to fall ill so you can avoid a fever. Is this not right?

---

[3]—Menón o de la Virtud (Sócrates VS. Menón)

A Foreigner—It is obvious that you presume it with irony; you know it is from my illness.

The Master—Young friend, you are mistaken if you think that I accept what you have granted to me before. Regardless, if you confirm that it is because of your illness, then I understand that you are mocking me or that our dialog has been an amusement.

A Foreigner—No, no! Not for a second, and much less in the state that I am in now. It simply happens that I am in the midst of a labyrinth where I do not have the slightest idea how to cross it. And I refer to having roamed the issue countless times, attempting not to fall into my usual faults, and as much as I try, I always return to the point of departure, which is the discomforting ideas that I should not reach; regardless of my purpose, I end up in a much further case from the start. It occurs that: I have discovered that, without the fear of being mistaken, the principal cause that subjugates me with great force is the fear to embarrassment itself. This evidently makes ideas discomforting and absurd, at the moment when I fear shyness, or isolated if I do not associate them with other thoughts, and we have concluded that those other thoughts cannot surely be deficient; since they provide and support the discomforting ideas, in order to obsessively perpetrate conjointly. Thanks to you, I have been able to identify and comprehend their true meaning. I have also noticed that the obsessive thoughts that support absurd ideas are: firmly believing that I am irrevocably condemned to remain in their dominion relentless of the wild fears, and they attach themselves with the suggestions of contempt and humiliation to myself and others; just like the vilest of men would be for having repented for his infamies.

The Master—It is not news to me that the majority of my activities I do out of affection towards you young people. It has now allowed for me to concede as true what is false, neither to keep the truth a secret. Fortunately, even though you are burdened by fear and you find yourself lost by displaying that we have walked in circles, I have to demand, making you see that you cannot display it to yourself or anyone, that the goal of fear is fear itself, and that there exist an eminent danger; the eminent danger of being omnipotent to fear itself.

A Foreigner—And with sincere affection, I thank you for your words, and without any apprehension let us move on. Frankly, I have wanted to justify that this is what mainly frightens me: not being able to stop its growth, which hastily augments in front of people to the point that it suppresses my control; similar to an obstacle that blocks a reflection, without giving an opportunity for reason to reach its own dominion.

The Master—The belief emerges at the end that its growth is uncontainable and accelerated. These ideas are what mainly make the purpose of fear. Is this not what you have deduced?

A Foreigner—It is what I can assume.

The Master—Completing these final ideas, they support the absurd thought of fearing shyness, by making themselves conjointly obsessive; provided that by themselves, they do not contain a pinch of significance.

A Foreigner—Yes. By themselves they ruin their task.

The Master—In all, the uncontainable growth and the fear of fear are the ideas that obsessively persuade you, and this is why you believe to be the last mortal in distress. This makes up the sum of the thoughts that insurmountably afflict you.

A Foreigner—And if perhaps I am not, what else is it that I feel?

The Master—Let us not pass the opportunity that you have opened in favor of our dialog and not to restrain from whatever you feel at this moment. Make an effort to answer what I am about to propose to you. Tell me: when fear grows, what happens to it, does it need something or nothing?

A Foreigner—What are you referring to?

The Master—What I am trying to say is, when fear grows, do the constitutive parts also grow and are affected? Or, are they not affected at all?

A Foreigner—They are also affected.

The Master—How are they affected? By chance, does fear augment without the augmentation of its pain?

A Foreigner—It is not possible.

The Master—And what will we say about the thought that judges and rejects pain and the undesirable. Is it affected as fear grows?

A Foreigner—It should be affected, right?

The Master—How so? Growing like a distressing pain?

A Foreigner—I do not know. It seems that it is a different thing.

The Master—And the distressing pain, in respect to the thought of fear, do they not correspond to each other when fear grows?

A Foreigner—In every moment. Otherwise it would not grow, nor would there be fear.

The Master—But, does it not occur that when one thing makes an impression on another, it is the norm that both things affect each other?

A Foreigner—Forcefully.

The Master—So, the thought that judges and rejects, and the distressing pain, do they mutually correspond to one another?

A Foreigner—Yes.

The Master—Then, the thought is affected even though it is not modified. Since it is not substantially modified, at least it is moved by the thought of danger or the unwanted. Is this not what proceeds?

A Foreigner—Strictly yes.

The Master—In all, will it be possible to believe in danger or what is not wanted, when it is perceived as imminent, or when it is believed as certain?

A Foreigner—Of course not. It is possible to know and even reject danger, or what is not loathed. As far as suffering by distressing pain, evidently not, and they are neither the beginning of the obsessive thoughts.

The Master—If after having investigated your answers, I believe that it is a ghost and not a real fruit, and if in such case I tear it off and throw it away, do not be frustrated with me and pretend that it is a present for you.

A Foreigner—And I beg to God that this maintains the attitude that has attached me to this path.

The Master—Quickly, let us define the path of the dilemma that I propose: When fear rapidly augments, it surges in a spontaneous and magical way, without affecting though; emanated by the fear of a threat that is not believed to be serious or imminent. Or, let us consent that it will only augment if its parts are also affected; this leads us to believe in the imminence and seriousness of a frightening or unwanted ill.

A Foreigner—Merely the last part. It is indispensable to accept the imminence and gravity of things that appear to me to be fearful, or unsettling, so that fear grows unrestrained; since a man, as lucid or as insane as he might be, does not exist who could fear without coincidentally believing in one of the things that are dreadful.

The Master—Excellent! From the things that cause you embarrassment or shyness, it is inferred that: your fear of embarrassment or shyness, will augment irrepressibly and hastily by believing in the imminence and seriousness of blushing, or in the imminence or seriousness of sweat; or by believing in the grave and imminent growth of fear; or by all of these at once. Subsequently, it is inevitable to be dismayed by being the most unfortunate of men. Is this not the effect?

A Foreigner—Once again I confirm this saying: "every resolved problems turns out to be trivial". Since I would not give a satisfactory answer if you asked me: why do I see everything, that you have now shown me to be absurd, so intricate?

In reality, I do not know that what comes to me is what is called a lake of lucidity, in the midst of madness, or I am leaving the dense forest; whether it is due to the last conjecture of our dialog, or by another matter. The case is that I clearly show myself that in order to fear, it is ineludibly required to be aware of a threat or unwanted things. Additionally, fear does not grow if the mind does not judge or understand the proximity or seriousness of danger. Clearing the cloud, the error that I constantly trip over denounces itself on its own, and it specifically consists of blindly believing that: fear is free to grow before its elemental parts are affected, or before receiving news of a threat or from anything that is repudiated; in a few words: fearing embarrassment without knowing the threat. This allows me to appreciate that blushing, the particularities, or bizarreness that I experience, even the discomforts that I provoke, are briefly identified as: the consequence of being afraid or terrorized. Let us finish by saying that the reflection of my fears is an effect of the fears and not its object. This is a significant addition to this subject.

With the purpose of attempting to group my most flaring thoughts, and perhaps to understand it better this way, we will explicitly place them in three separate groups. I will call the first, the absurd ideas, by being the ones that contains the most incoherent or abstract ideas that I could gather, or by being the ones that we studied at the beginning: the fear to the suffering of fear, or fear to a variant of itself, which is equally the fear of embarrassment or shyness. In the second group, I will place the ideas that, even though they lack meaning, they are not sustained by anything that is demonstrable or reasonable, they are: believing that I am impotent in overcoming embarrassment or shyness, in admitting the impossibility of containing the vicious spiral of countless fearful thoughts, or in the loss of dominion by the torments of embarrassment; but, with no limit to contain them, nor by the hope of death; with the trace of belief that death is not annihilation, but the perennial space where a conscious soul lives. The third, the thoughts that display themselves as the deduction of the last two, and are founded in: accepting to be destined to the irreversibly fatal, or to irremediable madness, even for seeing myself as infamous or vilely humiliated and abhorred, always by me and the entire world. With all the intricacies of the perverse influence of the three, I dare to opine that the first two are greatly persuasive. Regardless of their influence, each group tries to relate with the other or the other two, with such conformation that an affinity is a characteristic between them. Here, they follow each other without exception, and it is not viable to determine which one of the two takes the lead; with the fate that takes place in the inevitable outcomes, and the fatality of what is able to show who derives from whom. Hence, it is possible that the problem that most efficiently contributes to the vice of the obsessive thoughts derives from this.

Let us pretend that these groups were moving bodies, represented by three leather balls, and that pain joins them, similar to the equidistant belts that maintain the balls tied, all of them disposed in movement comparable to the planets in the solar system; whilst rotating around the sun, it does not leave its orbit but with the freedom that opposes restriction; they go in one director and another. Initially propelled by any of the two leaders, the third group follows next to it. The three move with the sluggishness and rapidity that imagination creates.

The Master—This digression I have not liked in the least. Let us leave a head to our conversation, so let us go forward to mark the road where the dense forest fools whoever ignores the natural traces that indicate orientation. Remember that the more time that passes, the sooner the ship will return, and it is my will to provide you with a guide that will allow you to support yourself.

A Foreigner—I cannot imagine that such unjust execution could take place. If the terms or authorities do not stop it, promise me that, before ending our dialog, we will talk about your thoughts in this respect. Let us say that I want to deepen the ideals that make you a man of faith of divine justice; and embrace them like a castaway who does not have anything else than an inflated rubber in the middle of the sea.

The Master—It is promised. Let me remind you that at the beginning of our dialog, it was you who mentioned that all the influx of my magic consisted of carrying orderly and methodical speeches. Whoever does not follow them throws himself into an unknown path; whilst the one that does follow them, will express exactly the essence of the object that your words refer to. Do you still keep this opinion?

A Foreigner—As bad as my memory could be, I will never forget what is fundamental.

The Master—In this occasion I mentioned that we should previously examine the matter that occupies the spirit, or the object that we propose and want to offer; keep in mind that it is the number one, and it means that unalterably proceeds the others. Therefore, if we want to hold on to the method, we will begin occupying ourselves in it. Furthermore, to deeply understand the object in question implies, from the start, to break it down and investigate it in a strict agreement. And attached to this I explain:

In the first step, it is precise to discriminate it from what it is not, which requires to possibly avoid more than an interpretation. For this, it is necessary to maintain a tendency of successful thoughts that go against the persistent vice of declaration with punctual faults; which means to avoid the tangled definitions, or excessive in words, or redundant explanations that lack meaning, likewise, ambiguous languages, or that, without discrepancy, act in two ways.

We have to tirelessly rectify them in order to reach the core of the problem, with the goal of understanding and faithfully manifesting it. And if it turns out to be indefinable, then we should at least formally establish it. With this concluded, we should finally be in a position to characterize the object, free from the bizarre or unnecessary, of what belongs to it, and it is not necessary to infer or bind; with the characteristic that allows us to describe the subject that it treats, but in a rigorous and concise condition; to know with laconic brevity.

The second step, if there is one, or if there is an object free from the opposition of reasoning that proves the contrary, or purely free from objections of judgment or common sense, and with time it proves to be indecipherable or enigmatic, in such case it will be necessary to analyze if the remaining object is simple or convoluted. It could be still indispensable to reduce it much more. Considering it a substrate, briefly, excluded from any accident or accessory, in its essence, independent from its state, quality, or qualities; to be able to see it removed from what accompanies or aggregates it by dependence. Now in its bare nature, we examine what makes it be what it is, and, if it has them, count its fundamental parts. In these terms, we will place our object and we will study its conduct as one, and if there are constitutive parts, how they relate amongst each other. Now, with this disposition and aware of its parts and behavior, we will see which one is active or passive, or which one could be greatly active or passive; given that the passive thing received the action of the agent without cooperating with it, it allows action by doing essentially nothing; whilst the active thing is effective in furnishing effect, or by acting in dilation.

For the third step it is necessary to study its properties, either active or passive, and if they are many, with a preference to those that are mainly active; so, it is necessary that the content in the second step develops entirely. It is at the end when we have to determine the situation or the circumstances in which the object is found, in relation to the other ones in its species, in order to highlight the important characteristics that make it peculiar, in comparison to any other of its nature. Additionally, to consider the changes that are inherent or inseparable and anything that influences it in a principal way. So, it will begin to take into account its behavior, even without ceasing from tending to the things where its affection falls, likewise, what mainly affects it such as the causing agents and anything that before being ceded precedes it. As said in brief, the object, causes and effects should be distinguished.

In this context, if by their difference the precedent faculties are identifiable, we will apply the fourth step. This will be to reinitiate the method with the novelty that now, by the object that takes the property or the most active quality, or that it predominates by its transcendence over the others, and after the second, go into the conclusive third, and successively until we are able to achieve what we have initially proposed in the intended subject. Understand that it will be done like this, if you do not pretend to dive in the detail of particularities, or complications will inevitably rise, with an infinite variety of aspects and nuances of things that are not vital.

On our way, we will count with a resource that, organized in four steps, will enable us to drive all effort determined to clarify and resolve what morally harms us, and is not easy to reveal. However, so that it feasible for many men to find what is not simple to penetrate, it is necessary to appropriate the discourses to the criteria and idiosyncrasy of the individual; in order to let the questionings and approaches be known, there are certain styles for certain people, whilst the same arguments and circumstances will move some, others will not understand them well. Consequently, the one that employs the method to carry the conviction to another, will be obliged to discern what better accommodates each one. For this, it is vital to know beforehand what his personality contains, or better to say what the biggest features of his personality that set him apart; this includes temperament, environment, education and what conditions, in a relevant way, the individual. Nearing towards the dialog, like the art of conversation alternatively requires; avoiding to, either through a question or response, lose the inference and prosecution. Is this not a direction that is opportunely oriented to come and go?

A Foreigner—It is impossible to say it better. Regardless, tell me, will it be a blunder to our dialog if we add a fifth step? With the goal that this last one be destined to point out the discovered error, once order is learned; in order to separate it from anything that can confuse it, hence, it will indicate with greater simplicity its position in the sequence of the things that favor bewilderment. Observe that I am living proof, at the cost of great suffering, of these horrible thoughts that with the figure of repetitive circles, can stop or sever. Even without presenting the evidence that provides certainty, I have enough experience to point out where they intervene, and for what reason they propitiate the vice that is suffered from, and why the mind does not pursue them more. Notice that only in this directive I have definitely interrupted that frightening circle of ideas that, analogous to a spiral, seem to attract me to Averno; with the enchantment that possesses a morbid fascination. And then, all its seduction loses its power in the moment when they submit; with the disdain when we abandon what, by lack of serious, does not raise interest, or when what results to be foolishness is despised. In similar terms, if decisively we do not believe in them, then they are definitively released.

The Master—It is not a blunder. The fifth step has a great purpose, when there is an error to reveal.

By being the son of a midwife I have learned its task, and it is exactly what I know how to do: to help give birth to the benefits that virtue provides, and I see that our dialogs have not been fruitless, that your studies are not vain, since you are capable of facing the impulses of irresistible fear, to the point that you make them resistible. I have not heard you mention anything about embarrassment or shyness. Have they simultaneously stopped from being invincible?

A Foreigner—Not as I have wished. It may seem as a lie that it deals with the same nature of the obsessive thoughts coupled to the impulses of irresistible fear; it has not been possible for me to overcome them. It is the case where there is no room to rest; there is no time to recognize the obsessive ideas. I ask myself, how is it possible to face an enemy that it is not identified? This motive keeps me ineludibly obliged to repeat, what I have lived many times, before the frightening attack of the obsessive ideas coupled to the impulses of fear. To be more explicit, I will try to describe it step by step, starting with the way that the phenomenon takes shape: imagine that these attacks are compared to the current of a river that descends dizzily, and drags us with thumping strength, that is only stopped by the depth of a gigantic and spectacular cascade; similar to Acheron, or river of pain, that leads to the world of the dead; therefore, we must avoid approaching the zenith of this helpless gap at any cost. This situation impulses us to want to escape with deaf desperation, that stuns the mind and blinds the senses, that makes us take useless actions; as if it was: allowing ourselves to be carried by the current, or to inversely fight and swim against it; in reality, the strength of the water drags us at every moment, sometimes more, sometimes less; even with the greatest effort, it is not possible to oppose the turbulent thrust, nor by alienating oneself with a conferred gift in order to refute frailty without inkling.

In such conditions it is evident that, from the obsessive thoughts coupled to the impulses of fear, no one is saved if they let themselves be dragged, nor wanting to resist them; the shore is reached by serenely swimming in the a direction that does not oppose the current. As long as it is this way, it is vital not to oppose it; not with the obstruction of guards at the entry of walled cities, having received an order to repel a multitude. On the contrary, with a serene and predisposed attitude to see them face to face, in a few words: in regards to them, in a mental predisposition that does nothing more than to contemplate them. This act of paying close attention to a particular thing is called meditation. For which, it is required to remain concentrated and not think of anything else, and not allow for anything that exists around us to make us lose our concentration.

It is important to emphasize the aforementioned, before an attack of obsessive ideas with irresistible impulses, far from the simplicity of maintaining an impassive attitude, in order to obtain the attention that the soul demands, ahead of the strength of the illness. Because of this fact, I should not reserve the caution that the obsessive ideas attack even if the individual is very skilled, and utilizes his resources with astonishing speed. Its sagacity is such, that it is not recommended to face it without knowing beforehand the positions, or better yet, the diverse meditations that are practiced, and how they should be exercised in advanced, and overall, to distinguish which ones and why it is necessary to avoid them. In sum, for the finale that we are searching for, it is necessary to talk about them. I will mention the most renown. Some of these have served so that great men achieved their maximum benefit.

A classification was recently presented that, due to its detail and focus, I consider being of great use. From here, I have taken two meditation groups that illustrate my objective. The first group is entitled: "Unrestrictive mental exercises"[4], which are, according to what the author mentions: "to concentrate on muscular and respiration relaxation". And he mentions that, "they are physical processes that are under voluntary direct control, whose practice includes the imagination of real and fantastic facts, aimed toward mental and physical relaxation".

---

[4]—Dinamica de la Rejalacion de Jonathan C. Smith

The second group is designated as: "Restrictive mental exercises"[4]. These comprise in their principle, to choose a stimulus or relatively simple subject that needs to be paid attention in a serene way; where the individual sees attentively, how the object of contemplation changes its appearance and develops independently; either by the project of daylight or by anything mobile. The object could be a plan, a sculpture, your hand, a musical piece, a character or a friend. It is here that it is attempted to deepen the comprehension of the object, employing the thought that is active and analytical. This part is called contemplation. A second part in the second group is called: "Meditation of centered concentration"[4]. It consists focusing on any single stimulus, such as a single image, the flame of a candle, the sound of the waves and allowing that it spontaneously repeats in the mind. Let us cite an example from the author: "Sit up straight, in a comfortable position, with your feet resting on the ground. Close your eyes if you wish, and take a few seconds to concentrate. With each breath, concentrate on the word 'one', and mentally repeat it, just like an echo. It is your only chore. Do not worry if your mind wanders off or is distracted; concentrate once again on the word". Contrary to what occurs in contemplation, there is no intention to take into account the word "one", and there is no way for this word to change or manifest itself. He adds that: "Meditation based on one stimulus, takes place with impartiality, and not waiting for anything"; it simply means to pay attention, and purely attention.

Lastly, within the second group it is also what is called: "Meditation of open concentration"[4], in which, the person slowly concentrates in any stimulus that exists in the mind

---

[4]—Dinamica de la Rejalacion de Jonathan C. Smith
[4]—Dinamica de la Rejalacion de Jonathan C. Smith
[4]—Dinamica de la Rejalacion de Jonathan C. Smith

and it eliminates it; which translates to tolerating, or clearly allowing for the stimulus to appear and disappear, and then wait for the subsequent one to emerge. He illustrates it in a clear example: "Imagine that you are in a forest at night, that you are resting in a tent. You feel tranquil and safe; you do not need to imagine anything. At ease, you listen to the sounds of the night, and you hear the wind that blows through the trees. Perceive the sound of the wind, and without thinking about it or without trying to imagine it, you continue once more to listen calmly. Now, feel the light and soft wind, register it, stop concentrating on what you have felt, and return into adopting a serene attitude". He clarifies that, in this open concentration, you do not need to understand the connection between each stimulus, there is no necessity of looking for profound meanings. Instead of paying attention to a word, sound or sensation, pay attention to the incessant flow of all the stimuli. Instead of listening to the wind, and specially the wind, pay attention to it, then the fragrance, then the sound of the birds, etc.; you are like a mirror, or like a clear lagoon that reflects everything that comes and goes, and you do not interfere. It is possible that you find yourself trapped by certain thoughts or distractions, you could follow them, attempt to reject them, be distressed or cornered by them. In this case, every time you are distracted, retake the task of meditation, serene and calmly, point out the distraction, and continue paying attention to any stimulus that comes to mind.

If it occurs that we see a better panorama of the meditation that I selected, it is then opportune to finalize my objective of this digression and retake the path.

Let us inquire about the practice of the aforementioned meditations for our case. The attacks of fear, or the obsessive ideas coupled with the irresistible impulses, are nothing more in meditation than: "the stimulus to continue". What do we wait to occur if we want to face the attack of such a formidable enemy? A contemplative meditation, belonging to the group of restrictive mental exercises, whose characteristic is to exercise an stimulus in order to pursue it and see it change with the help of thought. This is the precisely the attitude that our diabolical stimulus needs to swallow us into its macabre spiral; dependently, it wants us to follow it. In order not to be overwhelmed, it is this contemplative meditation that we need to infallibly avoid.

With the group of nonrestrictive mental exercises, naturally it would not be practical to attempt to imaginatively concentrate in any part of the body, or any other thing, since it is precisely what our stimulus does not consent; on the other hand, it tends to drag us where we do not want to go. In all, it is easy to infer that, in a meditation of open concentration, we would not be in a position to change the stimulus of our will, since we have assimilated it punctually, the fight consists of getting rid of it, and even though I have said it, I reinforce it: without running away, without abhorring, without insisting, without analyzing or pretending to know if we are following it, or it is following us; summarily, it is with this order that the mind allows us to see with sufficient clarity, in order to provide us with a simple explanation of what is happening to us; then, we are correctly meditating before the frightening ghost. This is corroborated when we know that, by not searching for it with anticipation, we observe its presence without being led by it.

In conclusion, the position that is given to us to face the fearsome horrors is the meditation of centered concentration that belongs to the second group of mentally restrictive exercises. However, if it has merely been exercised, it is not simple to find in our mind the thoughts of fear at the moment when they begin; it seems as if they hold the ability to be imperceptible. Before, by the practice and firm position, it attenuates the activities of sick thoughts. I affirm without hesitation that, in order to not involuntarily return to the river or to be tangled by the fatal circle of obsessive ideas, the disposition of an attentive mind is imperative; with the same fluency in which something that is clear and alive is in the palm of our own hand. Nonetheless, I sustain that it is neither the knowledge nor the intellectual operation that lets go of the fearful ideas in a definitive way, instead the meditation we are speaking about. This is what definitely prevents the absurd ideas from attaching to others, or the impulses of fear; without giving space to the insistence of error or distraction. Ostensibly, fear disappears when the thoughts pass the judgment of fear toward the isolated idea, though meditation. Where the isolated idea or ideas are: the absurd ideas that do not attach themselves to fear anymore.

Let us provide an expression that means the limit of fear, and call them "frontier ideas"; by being the ideas that have broken the link with fear or terror; by not allowing the succession in the spiral of ideas coupled to suffering, or when it has broken the belts of the leather balls; not because they do not allow the continuity to the general thought, instead because they thwart the obsession that belongs to pain. In other mental conditions that are perhaps less sickening, we find the frontier ideas to the maximum—or precisely in the concept of faith, or by the memory of knowledge, that similarly act as splitting or breaking the continuity of certain sentiment that has provoked a problem or alienation. I believe that, it is similar to the case where the mind changes impulses for impulses, especially a passion for another of greater magnitude; which could be verified when a kleptomaniac is forced to abstain by a cruel and fearsome dictator; the thief transposes the impulse to rob as an impulse of fear.

It has been a confirming fact for me to recall the frontier ideas, just like the reasoning that they took me to. It has allowed me to recuperate the appeasement that I drastically lost in more than one occasion, by finding myself in particularly stressing situations; we can judge with the perspective that I saw it very dramatically at a certain moment; but on those that I unforgivingly would have remained, or until I did not ingest an anxiolytic that stopped the attacks. And I do not want to omit or hide that, having contracted the "classic dengue", this was my behavior during one of the worst times I have lived as a consequence of this illness. So, if I took the hand of the drug (15 drops of clonazepam only), it was because on that unfortunate night, I awoke by opening my eyes with the agility that wakefulness interrupts a horrible nightmare, and our soul alerts us of the approaching of an angry beast; it resembled a being composed of a nature that does not begin, and whose attack is sudden. Quickly, I took the weapons of knowledge and I obstructed its path until I conquered the tranquility that allows us to achieve sleep once more. I fell asleep with the satisfaction of having made the monster disappear. Minutes later, while I was asleep, the contention resumed with the impetus that is capable of. Surprised, I reincorporated myself. In the midst of this trance, I diverted my thoughts and began to believe that I would suffer the same fate as King Pyrrhus II, when he declared war against the Romans; who won at the cost of major loses, which also contributed to his deterioration, to the point that he ended at the mercy of them. Then, with a weak body and a soul influenced by the febrile illness, and without wanting to recall anymore the frontier ideas, I fled and dragged fear with me. In order to find refuge in one of my last resources, convinced that I will never find self-control, it would have been preferable if I took the tranquilizer under medical supervision. I humbly recognize that, that night, I completely lost the battle by having turned my back on reason and repressing my will. However, this battle did not mark the end or the premonition of the end of my efforts. Perchance, years later, with the determination to try the benefits of homeopathy, I decided to retire from the anti-depressants that I continuously ingested the last 10 to approximately 20 years of my battle with depression (could have been the selective inhibitors of the reuptake of serotonin and noradrenaline).

Close to a month and a half of having suspended my ingestion of them, the attacks of terror came over me, or if you prefer, the ideas with impulses of irresistible fear; this time, they were disguised in a dream where I found myself trapped, without hope, in a tight a dark tunnel, so tight that it was not possible to move my body or to ingest air. I abruptly awoke escaping the nightmare, and I instantly understood that my old antagonist would not stop its attack; I felt its stubborn presence trying to penetrate in order to dissuade me from regaining control, at the moment in which my frailty, or distraction, would allow it to drive me off path. I say penetrate, when we feed with our imagination these obfuscating ideas, forgiving and spoiling them with an imagination that grows them in no time at all. It could have been the experience acquired from the previous confrontation, and at that time, anticipated the disposition of maintaining my thoughts clearly, it is the reason why I did not concede neither distraction nor any reservation until I did not domesticate it.

This last onslaught gave me the confidence to extend the contention; to not limit my effort to face the attack solely because every excuse exhausted; dissipating the impression that the mind induces in order to evade the enemy, called phobias or panics. I was attracted to the idea that at any path I would bump into it.

After 40 days of having gotten rid of my body such anti depression medication, and without distancing myself from the homeopathic medication, the horror attacks reappeared with a reproduction without precedent. Regardless of the unusual, I was able to mitigate them most of the time; recuperating control and self-confidence. However, as much as I tried to remain attentive to the obsessive ideas with impulses of insurmountable fear, there were moments when to release them implied a prolonged and inexhaustible encounter; by having naively forgotten that: "it is necessary not to prioritize the mentioned attacks, a maxim or any other idea"; as if it dealt with a shield in order to not be harmed; given that, it returns against oneself, with the invariable persistence of a body that is reflected by a mirror each time it passes in front of it. And the idea in question was concretely that: "it is feasible to eliminate the error without it harming, except in the lapse that gives a start, as long that it has the clarity of the ideas that it has been associated with"; in this way, only the abilities that is reached with practice is lacking. Albeit, this concept does not seem to be a mistake, it is a repeated reminder; falling in the error by pretending that dominion of oneself consisted of being more insistent than the obsessive ideas; in reality, it is the way where obscurity moves us. In this way, I once again confused the act of being attentive with the thought that I should be attentive and patient to any attack. To not proceed like this, guarantees confusion and defeat; a named concept, reasoning, or any other thought, as sublime or imminent as it is, reverts against me and unquestionably dissuades me into believing that it is impossible to suppress terror. Then, suggested that there is nothing that could stop the obsessive ideas with impulses of irresistible fear, it is the worst of my infernos.

Attempting not to fall in the aforementioned error, during the course of an entire afternoon, I restrained the attacks. However, the internal unease, even though it was tolerable, it was so uncomfortable that nothing seemed pleasant; with the uneasiness that fear provides in a space that is incipient. It is a state of mood that is undeniably produced by a confrontation inconclusive and deficient, by the lack continuity in concentration; where the sickening thoughts, that are associated with the impulses of fear, cleverly penetrate and recuperate the lost territory. By night time, and greatly due to an effort in my part, calmness came to me completely. However, after two hours of having been asleep, I awoke with the fixed idea that I would return to the brawl, and after a few more seconds, the cleverly disguised announced attack reinitiated;

I believed by its constant repetition, that it advanced with the speed that proliferates a cancer that invades the entire body; since it was more confusing to identify the sickening ideas every time, even though I remained attentive. Completely convinced, and having lost all hope to resist the subsequent battles, I took one a half tablets, of 4.5 mg, of Bromazepam; similar to someone who looks for refuge at the point where the defensive lines of his army have been devastated by the enemy. The following morning, I awoke without the desire to reflect or analyze, I only thought about the most appropriate drug to protect me. Suddenly, the answer came like a lightening volt. I had fallen in deceit, more simple than certain, it was not founded in anything else than: "in believing that my malady advanced, in the virtue that it would be difficult to identify the obsessive ideas coupled to the impulses of irresistible fear"; when the only fearsome thing is precisely this same idea; that is to say that it requires that I believe in it, since by itself it is unsustainable, and not because these sickening thoughts are not very perceivable. And in respect to suffering from an illness that unquestionably advances, it does not mean that said news deorbits me at the moment when I recall or hear it; it is indispensable that there exists a chemical unbalance in my brain. From the aforementioned, I understood that these obsessive ideas possess three principle abilities:

1st—They are extremely repetitive.
2nd—They engage with such speed, that they almost do not allow us to stop and observe them.
3rd—They are so versatile, that they fool us whilst disguised by countless facets, although they do not have any other object than to dissuade us from being able to control them.

If we add that they are also capable of combining the three, we have to admit that, figuratively, it deals with a formidable being. It happens that it is inevitable to be fooled by it whilst using reason and memory. At this point it is advised to write in a piece of paper, or memorize with clarity, the ideas that go through one's head with great intensity, during an attack of terror, but restraining from wanting to analyze or search for an answer, or from setting forward maxims, ideas, concepts, reasoning, or arguments; only with an attentive attitude, with the exclusive goal of seeing these obsessive thoughts, with the clarity which we see something in the palm of our own hand. Subsequently, we should do nothing less than remain attentive to its incomparable and particular insistence.

I had to wait merely one night to corroborate these observations. It was then when I awoke from one of those nightmares where I am boxed in the abyss; in the eternity of the dead, more conscious of the dimension and time; it overcame, announcing with the blood that throngs in my nape, the cold sweat, and me perceiving it at the door, I remained attentive; as someone who is waiting for an interesting piece of news; waiting for the first intense thoughts of penetrating panic, of the obsessive ideas coupled to the impulses of irresistible fear, of the intense sickening ideas that drag and precipitate me into a deranged fugue. And against all fatality, I do not cross the door, given that I did not feel any fear. I did not even take notice when it took place, even after feeling the intuition in my bones that I would be attacked with its greatest power. Surprised, I noticed that the ingrained malady did not prosper; in the same form that it does not transmit the force that breaks the links of a chain, and without succession, those leather balls representing the morbid ideas, they are lost when the belt breaks. And knowing that it deals with an obstinate contender, I did not want to be taken by surprise, and I continued with the same attitude until I would find myself tranquil, or until feeling free from the apparitions of the sickening thoughts. In complete tranquility, I was able to surmise over the nature of the obsessive ideas coupled to the impulses of irresistible fear:

a) They can attack with great success without being repetitive.
b) As long as the frontier ideas are not discovered, the obsessive ideas are capable of imprinting fear or dread.
c) It is not possible for them to penetrate if they are deprived from their habitual persecution of rapid thoughts.

God willing, my suffering and observation will not go unnoticed, and that having been studied will serve for their veracity. As far as what represents me, this knowledge is undoubtedly a great help, a gift from heaven. Yet, it is difficult for me to live attentively, which involves being constantly with anxiety and restlessness; dealing with insomnia, nightmares, premonitions that something bad is about to happen; led by a distracted imagination that begins to admit the nearing of a stalking predator, which restlessly and patiently waits for any type neglect in order to attack, and it continues succeeding in its purpose the least incipiently; although, in the worst of cases, I have felt the urge to face it, until completely stopping its implacable advance of horror; even with this, I am incited to ordinarily believe that: in this occasion, I will not be successful.

By the sum of all the disorders that I have discussed, I resolved to resume taking antidepressant; to give my body the component that I do not properly produce (serotonin and noradrenaline) and to reestablish the calmness and vitality that such drugs provide.

How could I not recall the enormous admiration that that night caused, to show myself the power that has been granted to us in order to be sound in the face of great nervous excitations; without being harmed by the most insignificant emotional imbalance. It is not surprising that, this wonderful conquest propelled my determination to sink into the phenomenon known as claustrophobia. And having attempted to willfully submit myself to confined spaces, not without paying the price of intense agitation, I was able to enrich my experience by deducing two infallible principles for anyone who has not practiced focused meditation in self-control, and is victim of phobias:

A) To know and previously identify the coupled ideas to the impulses of terror.

B) To be attentive, in order to wait for the progression of such obsessive ideas; subsequently, to think about meditation, is to lose concentration.

Otherwise, it is not feasible to find oneself serene, without suffering from anxiety or desperation.

Conclusively, I am planning to straighten up what I misconceived about social phobia, due to the fact that I did not understand how to contain it; given that, there is no mental rest when the senses are set to listen, or thinking about speaking; because, wanting to concentrate with constant cessation or deviation from attention, it certainly seemed to me to be undoable to stop its onslaught. I would think that: without being attentive, I would never see the frontier ideas pass! But I now know that, if the obsessive ideas coupled to social fear, they should be clarified with anticipation, in order to posteriorly perceive them, in a state that does not require any mental operation, or stumbling block to recognize the presence of the frontier ideas; given that it does not obligate me to enact two mental operations at the same time, which would truly be impossible. On the contrary, ceasing from attending a talk or to be around a social event, it will predispose me to distraction; therefore, my mind would deviate towards things I fear, and ponder on anything that would favorably dominate me.

Ultimately, the closed cell of resignation has opened so I am not with my arms crossed, since the anti-depressants represent a great help, they are not a panacea that remedies by perfectly eliminating the effects of these affections. The medications luckily give us the quality of life, but they do not cure us, they exclusively control us; and I refer to the fact that, even with the use of the current medication and with an adequate dose, there are lapses where its benefits disappear, leaving us without protection; provided in certain cases to the physiology of each individual, or by medicinal interactions, or by effects of a previous illness that unbalances the chemicals responsible of emotions. Likewise, it could be because of external factors where the circumstances exceed any type of prevision, or are inevitable, or by being psychologically adverse to the things that patient considers important, and that we are permanently exposed until the end of our life. Let us not talk about the many cases where the wrong medicine was prescribed, since, in order to prescribe the adequate dose, it is a natural prerequisite to particularly administer each patient; based on the principle that each organism, without disregarding those from its own species, is not identical to the others, which implies to administer a prescription and appropriate dose to each person. There are some that require the maximum recommended dosage, whilst some only require the minimum. In all, there are times in which said medication does not offer any benefits to the patient, and they call him a refractory patient. Beware! In this facet it is easy to mistaken a refractory patient to one that was wrongly diagnosed.

Having taken nine types of antidepressants (all from the fourth generation, or reuptake of serotonin) throughout 10 years, and under care and psychiatric prescription, I have still not seen any drug that completely mitigates my social phobia. It could have been by chance or by the urgencies of destiny, but after having practiced the aforementioned deductions, I finish by setting three premises that allow me to overcome myself in front of people:

1st—Identify in advance the thoughts that alter, or make us abstain from the encounter; which has commonly been that: it is very difficult to remain attentive, albeit disguised by many figments or occurrences to confuse me.

2nd—To conserve a passive attitude or intellectual rest, that has nothing more to do than wait for the ideas that grab us.

3rd—To know that the greatest dominion is reachable, suppressing the impulses of fear, not so with the blushing, or sweating, or any other bizarre manifestation of the human body, or an opinion that belongs to us or others, and that its off reach to our will.

Thanks to the daily interactions with people, I have verified that without any contradictions to this respect, the more attentive that I am in front of people, the more calm that I feel. To my misfortune, this is precisely the crux where the most radical of my defects lives, the beginning of my complications and the continuity of my deficiencies. And due to the importance of this, I have precisely inquired into the profound meditational exercises or Buddhist meditation; I am very interested in it, since multiple demonstrations assure that practicing it allows the development of ample lapses of concentration, with an extraordinary self-control that does not require of frontier ideas. This implies that the self-control does not have pain, or wounds or any sensation of distress, or any irreducible manifestation of fear.

Such conceptions have directed me to a point where the philosophy that judges and analyzes has ended, in order to continue in the path of the philosophy that confines in meditation, excluding every exam or reasoning. We are now talking about the philosophy of the Buddha, of the wise men that, with enough training, have reached levels that they called: "to empty the content of conscience, in order to be filled by reality", and they succinctly point out that: "the illusion ceases, reality remains"; a mental and physical state where a maxim of dominion and plenitude is conquered. Having subdued the intrinsic illusion of human beings, and of the rest that we are a slave to; which are widely labeled as: obsession, frustration, sadness, fear, ambition, hate, vanity, etc.; although they purely mirages, by which, in the eyes of someone that is "initiated", the passions vanish. It is said that such exercise is practiced daily, similar to a profession, even without expecting any material remuneration for their effort. They show us that, by this permanent activity, it is possible to obtain the ability to go from thoughts to the quietude of observation, with the objective of annulling the spiritual and corporal sufferings. Such is the case of one of the men of invaluable greatness who, having been the son of princesses, despised wealth and power, and had the divine inspiration to initiate himself in the path of virtue. He left us a few words for anyone who aspires to follow his steps: "The first thing that must be learned is to listen with a tranquil heart, an open and attentive soul, without passion or desire, without opinion, without judgment". He also suggests that: "Thoughts and feelings are good things that should be heard, without paying excessive or minimal amounts of attention, and to surprise the interior voice through them; a voice that governs the eagerness of the illuminated. The last human perfection is reached through the art of listening, forgetting yourself, in order to cease from tending to the clamors of suffering and pain, and sharpening the senses". Then, the fondest of his disciples approached him and said: "Wisdom that gives illumination is not transmitted; knowledge can be communicated but not wisdom. It is necessary to live it, but as far as discuss it or teach it, no! It is not possible! These words serve a bad purpose to the mysterious road of doctrine". He says: "I am going to confess to you that have I sinned with lust, concupiscence, and vanity, only by living in the most embarrassing desperation, I was able to stop my eagerness and passions; so much pain it cost me to love the true world, not to confuse it with the one imagined and wished by me, nor with the genre of perfection that my spirit represented, I learned to take it just like it is, to love it and be part of it; the way to live and act has the most weight than the dialogs. Greatness does not reside in dialog or thought, rather in the acts". In other instances they refer to it preaching with this clarity: "The world is filled with suffering to mankind, since its mind is filled with fantasy and its heart finds itself saturated with desire and ambition. Men perceive reality through the filter of the illusion, this is why they are led to believe in the fiction that they themselves elaborate and they accept them as true. This is how truth can be led to an error, and this error leads to many others to become illusory truths; all this can be satisfactory for a time, but at the end, the only things that are found are tribulation, anxiety and misery". And he synthetizes by expressing the following: "When ambitions cease, liberty begins. When the fire of hate is extinguished and illusions fade, the false beliefs, and the conditions that cloud the mind, then liberty is reached". It is ultimately interesting to find that this system is not of religious nature; given that superior entities do not intervene as mediators, in order to sublime the spirit or to dilute the fondness that excites us. This explains why Buddhism tolerates anyone who thinks different, by being comprehensive to the principles and adaptability, of the practitioner, during the stages of spiritual progress. Also, it also puts emphasis on anything that obstructs development, and to anything we can fall captive to, by displaying things that boast them and proceed with prepotency; and it specifically charges it to the extraordinary powers or to the contact with superhuman characters; given that they deviate us whilst wanting to find the refuge and an explanation in them, losing the path in the quest for the truth.

By this succinct, I attempt to not stray from what always is exposed to the impairment of time (26 centuries), I have wanted to attach myself to its most loyal followers. In these days they receive the name of monks of Zazen. These masters, then and now, have demonstrated with the example of the entire world, to what point it is possible for human beings to achieve the dominion of the body and soul.

With nothing better for me to deepen in thought, let us begin to find out what is Zen, with the words of the master Deshimaru: "the secret of Zen consists of sitting down, without any goal or profiting spirit, in a position of great concentration This uninterested form of sitting down is called Zazen; Za means to sit, and Zen to meditate"[5]. He adds: "the practice of Zazen is the great efficiency for the health of the body and spirit; since the spinal cord stands, and levels the just tension of the muscles and calms the agitation of the superficial layers of the brain, without shunning reality away. To be attentive is the then and now; what is now important is the present, taking into account the acts, words or thoughts, without thinking in the past or future, and forgetting the instant present; it deals with overcoming, with practice, all the forms of thought. Zen cannot be framed in a concept, it needs to be practiced; it essentially is an experience. The practice of Zazen is only concentration in the position of the body, in the way we breathe and the attitude of the spirit".

It is not my wish to detail the position of the body, since I have not exercised yet, but I have opened the doors of hope with the advice of the master Zen, who explains that: "respiration plays a primordial role by establishing a slow, powerful and natural rhythm, so we should concentrate in a soft, long and

---

[5]—La Práctica del Zen

profound respiration; this comes in a natural form. The correct exercise neutralizes the nervous shocks, superimposing to the instincts to the passions and controlling the mental activity, to the point that the cerebral cortex rests, and the conscious flow of thoughts ceases, producing a sensation of wellbeing and serenity. Sitting in Zazen, allows us to run through the images and thoughts that go through the subconscious, such as clouds through a clear sky; without opposing to them, without grabbing on to them; allowing them to pass like shadows in front of a mirror. And the profound subconscious is reached, much further from all thought. The true Zen is practiced without motivation, without finality, without searching for the self-control of thought, with nothing to obtain, nothing to think about, truth does not need to be searched for, and we do not have to run away from the illusion. We only have to be present, here and now, sitting in silence. When someone is sick, weak, sad, or concentrated in their little self, inspiration is accentuated in respiration, and this abates even more the body. Practicing the contrary would enable receiving the true energy; if the expiration is just, inspiration is automatically made, subconsciously (without cutting expiration). This method if respiration is the basis of health".

For my part, I have faith in this philosophy; however, I have a few doubts: how should I behave in order to not lose concentration? I also found a precise response in his book, when he talks about this same problem: "Frequently, during Zazen, thoughts rise ceaselessly. Quotidian problems, desires, anxiety, they attack us continuously. We should not fight against them, nor cling to them. Our spirit is complicated, difficult to guide, and agile like a monkey; if we try to dominate it, we will fall in the account that it is impossible. However, the practice of Zazen makes us gradually abandon preoccupations, the external attractions, such as the whisper of the wind, the sound of cars and the singing of birds. There exist diverse mediums that favor this concentration; for example, to strongly tighten the abdomen during respiration. Beginners should initially correct concentration and form; they will later gradually improve subconsciously".

Lastly, he gives reference of where and on whom electroencephalograms were made, which reveal a cerebral cortex in complete relaxation, and an enhancement and regularization in the activity of the function in the neurovegetative system, linked to the activity of the profound subcortical (under the cerebral cortex) structures, during the practice of Zazen. He explains his own experience: "Profound meditation practically detains conscious thought, and our conscience becomes peaceful, tranquil, and receptive. Then, the kept posture and profound respiration create an environment where there is no thought or suffering; one lives in the depth of one's self, where everything is empty and in absolute silence, and the roots are cut of any suffering and desire. So, it is important to be in a silent room, and have sober meal and beverages, also to reject any commitment or business". He concludes with these maxims: "True wisdom is much further than personal intelligence. True wisdom, our intuition, should be created through the normal and original condition of the conscience in Zazen. It is not important to believe or know what is substantial, or what is the cause and effect, instead to understand the phenomenon here and now, how we should be and how we should live".

It was not my intention to cover so many things without going in depth into any of them. I recognize that I left on our path many questions that I was not able to fathom, but to simply glance at them. Amongst them, there is one in particular that I have not forgotten; on the contrary, I was going to carry it to the end of my road. It is precisely my fear of death. However, it is not the one that intuits as the most perfect state of annihilation, instead as the incontrollable fear that dread makes us believe. There are few things that by opposition surpass my preconception, and one of them is the conversation that Aristotle would name: "The inventor of the moral science", moments before his execution. It is my wish to end with the words that correspond to one of his most illustrious biographers"

"For my part, I have despised what the vast majority of men esteem, and I do not understand any other guide than the truth. I will do anything I can to live and die, when the time has come, as virtuous as it is possible. I invite everyone, and I invite you, to adopt this lifestyle and to fight this fight. After having distinguished myself in the battles of Potidaea, Anphipolis and Delium, it is in itself the most interesting fight of any other in the world. Serve yourself from the light of this conversation, which allows us to see that the best course that we can take is to live and die in the practice of justice and the rest of the virtues. Let us march down the road that it outlines for us, and let us commit the others to imitate me"[6].

When he was presented in front of the judges with the charge of corrupting the youth, his death sentence, he told them: "Athenians, fearing death implies believing that we are wise without being it, and believing to know what is unknown. In effect, no one knows death, or knowing if it is the greatest benefits for man. However, it is feared as if it was known with certainty that it is the greatest of the ills. Ah! Is it not embarrassing ignorance to believe to know something that is unknown? In respect to me, Athenians, perhaps I am much different than the rest of men when it comes to this. If I seem to be wiser, it is because, without knowing what awaits us after death, I say and sustain that I do not know. What I know to be certain is that to commit injustices, disobey whoever is better and is above us, whether it is God or men, is the most

---

[6]—Apologia de Socrates

criminal and embarrassing; therefore, I will not ever fear or escape the ills that I do not know, and which can be truly good; but I will always fear and escape ills that I know with certainty to be truly bad"[6].

The last moments of his life he spent discussing philosophy, and being surrounded by his regular disciples. Although Plato was not present that day, he refers to the tale of this group of friends: "By seeing and listening to him with so much faith, he seemed to be a blissful man who would not die without the protection from God. We did not feel the pleasure that ordinarily mixed itself into our conversation; we felt a rare mixture of pleasure and pain, when we began to consider that in a moment he would abandon us. We did not stop seeing him even for one day; we ordinarily spent the entire day with him. The day of his execution, we got together much earlier. We had known the night before, whilst leaving the prison the night before, that the ship had returned from Delos. On that day, the mayor told us to wait in the entrance, because The Eleven[7] ordered for the irons to be removed from Socrates, giving the order that he is to die today. At our entrance, we found him with Xanthippe, his wife, who had one of his children in her arms. After Socrates asked his friend Crito to take her home, who was sobbing, we continued, as we were accustomed, talking about philosophy, and without anyone wanting to bring the subject, he spoke like this:

Socrates—There could not be a more convenient occupation for a man that will cease to live soon, than to inquire about that same voyage. What better thing can we employ ourselves until sunset?

---

[6]—Apologia de Socrates
[7]—The magistrates in charge of the oversight of the prisons.

Cebes—Socrates, those that affirm that it is not permitted to commit suicide, what do they base themselves on? I have heard many say that it is bad, but I have not heard anything that will satisfy this point.

Socrates—Youngsters, what I have heard could seem irrational, but it is not due because it lacks ground. I do not want to argue that the greatest lesson in the mysteries is that each one of us is in this world limited to a position where it is prohibited to abandon without permission. This maxim is too elevated and it is not easy to penetrate everything that it locks. But, here is one that is more accessible, and that it seems to me to be unanswerable: is it not true that men belong to God?

Cebes—Very true.

Socrates—Yourself, if one of your slaves takes his life without your permission, would you not be completely furious towards him?

Cebes—Without a doubt.

Socrates—For this reason, it is fair to sustain that there no motive to commit suicide, and that it is precise that God sends a formal order to die, much like the one that he has sent to me on this day.

Cebes—What you say seems probable, but you mentioned that the philosopher presents himself happy towards death, and this seems bizarre if it is true that men belong to God, unless you truly believe that you will find better citizens in the other world.

Socrates—I could perhaps hope of it in this respect, however, I will confess why I am not so afflicted in these moments, hoping that there is something reserved for men after life, and that according the old maxim, the good will be better treated than the bad. Beforehand, let us see what Crito has to tell us. It seems that for some time he has been trying to talk to us.

Crito—Why is it that if you do not know what is death, you house a profound hope that it is something good, given that it is precisely one of two things: one, death is an absolute annihilation; a deprivation of all feeling, a peaceful sleep that is not disturbed by any dream, or that it is a voyage of the soul from one place to another. Perhaps to where the judges of eternity are, making true justice. Are you not mistaken by saying that death is a great good?

Socrates—It is now opportune that I expose to you the reasons that I have for a man, who has consecrated his entire life to philosophy, to die entirely and in serenity: It would be ridiculous that after continuing on without a break, during my entire life, a preparation to confront death and having advised you that wisdom does not consist of explaining the world, rather to fabricate a refuge of tranquility with the few things that you can give to it, fearing and distrusting it. What is the motive to wish to die and that I am worthy of death? Let us see if you think like me. Do you think that the vast majority of men think that the one who does not have pleasure in things such as eating, drinking, love, attire, and the rest of adornments of the body that he does he does not take advantage of, does not know how to truly live; and believe that the one who does not enjoy the pleasures of the body, is very close to death.

Simmias—It is true.

Socrates—And you, do you believe that the true philosopher should cherish or despise them, as long as necessity does not force them to rely on them?

Simmias—He cannot do anything less than despise them.

Socrates—Then, all the watchfulness of a philosopher does not have the body as an objective, but on the contrary, the soul?

Simmias—Most probably.

Socrates—So, from all these things that I have just finished discussing, it is evident that what is proper and peculiar to a philosopher is to work more peculiarly than the rest of the men, on releasing his soul from the commerce of the body.

Simmias—It is true.

Socrates—And what will we say about the body when it is associated to the inquiry of science? I will explain it to you through an example: sight and hearing, have a type of certainty, or the poets are correct in their songs by telling us that we truly do not hear or see. Given that if these two senses are not secure, the others would be much less, since they would be weaker. Do you believe it like I do?

Simmias—Yes, without a doubt.

Socrates—Then, when does the soul finds the truth? Because whilst it looks for it with the body, we clearly see that this body beguiles it, and it induces it to error.

Simmias—It is true.

Socrates—Is it not better if the soul is not disturbed by sight, or by hearing, or pain, or pleasure; and when in itself, abandons the body, without maintaining any relation to it, when this becomes possible, noticing the object of its inquiry in order to get to know it?

Simmias—You are right.

Socrates—And is it not like when the soul of a true philosopher depreciates the body, and does whatever it is necessary to free himself from its distractions. He does nothing more than to fool the soul in the quest for the truth, which he always has the smallest relationship with.

Simmias—You are right.

Socrates—This principle follows that whilst we have our body, and our soul is sunk in this perturbation, we will very difficultly possess the truth. In effect, our body presents us with thousands of obstacles by obligating us to provide it with nourishment, for the illnesses that ensue and that blind our inquiries. On the other hand, it fills us with love, desires, thousands of chimeras and all kinds of needs. And where do wars, seditions, and combats stem from? From the body with all its passions. Is it not true that wars proceed from the anxiety to pile up wealth, and do not we feel pressed to pile it up as a result of the body, to serve as a slave to its demands? This shows us that, in general, there is no concession to think about philosophy. Lucky, the greatest of our ills takes place in the act to make us think, and suddenly in these moments, the body internes to distract us from our inquiries. If it is possible to know the truth, whilst we live with our bodies, two things could happen: truth is never known, or that it is known after death, once the soul is free from material weight and it belongs to itself; until God comes to free us from that impulses that infect us.

Simmias—Surely.

Socrates—If it is exactly as I have mentioned, every man that is able to be in the situation that I find myself in, has the greatest basis to hope that the other side must better than any other place, he will possess what we search with so much work in this world. So, this voyage, that I have been subjected to, fills me with sweet hope. I ask you: does not this separation and freedom, constitute the entire occupation of a true philosopher?

Simmias—That is what it seems to me.

Socrates—Subsequently, the true philosopher trains for death, and it does not seem in anyway terrible. Think of it yourself. Ah! My dear Simmias, you must believe that you will go with the greatest pleasure.

Simmias—By Zeus! It is a complete extravagance.

Socrates—And do you not think that strength and temperance, which are only known by name by the majority of people, are the virtues that consist of not being a slave to your desires, instead to be superior to them, and to live in moderation?

Simmias—How would I not?

Socrates—And if you want to examine the strength and temperance of others, you will find that they are ridiculous.

Simmias—Why?

Socrates—Because the vast majority of men believe that death is one of the terrible ills. And when men that call themselves strong, undergo death with some valor, they do not suffer from it, instead they see it a greater ill.

Simmias—I agree with that.

Socrates—Then, men are strong as a result of fear. And is it not a ridiculous thing that men are brave by fear, or strong by shyness?

Simmias—You are right.

Socrates—So, these same men that call themselves moderate or temperate, are so by intemperance. Although, it may seem impossible at first sight, it is the result of this crazy and ridiculous temperance; from a precedent in which they renounce a pleasure by the fear of seeing themselves deprived from other pleasures that they desire, and that they are submitted to. They call intemperate those who are dominated by passions, but at one point they do not overcome certain pleasures, but other passions to which they are submitted or subjugated to. This assimilates the aforementioned that they are temperate and moderate by intemperance.

Simmias—It seems very true.

Socrates—This means that strength, temperance, justice, prudence, in one word, wisdom, is true and independent from the pleasures, the sadness, fears and the rest of the passions. Whilst, without this virtue, it is only the transaction of some passions with others; they are nothing more than shadows of virtue, virtue slave to vice that has nothing truthful or healthy. True virtue is a purification of all sorts of passions; and there are many signals that make believe that those that established the purifications were not despicable people, who in my opinion have effectively philosophized. If my efforts have not been useless, and if I have achieved it, I hope by God's will to know it in brief. Here it is my friends, my apology, and the reason why I am not sad or deprived of appeasement; rather with the hope that I will find a better life.

When the moment arrived, he drank with a firm hand the poison that he was to drink in order to abide to the death sentence that was imposed by the Athenian tribunal; for corrupting the youth through his dialogs.

Crito, with tears in his eyes, added, "Socrates you died undeservedly", to what Socrates responded, "If I would not have done it, I would have deserved it".

With the same serenity that he used to dialog with his disciples, he lay on his bed, covered himself with a blanket, and waited for death under it. It began thought his feet, and slowly rose; just as he described that he lost the sensibility in his feet and posteriorly his legs. Finally, the light that illuminated his mind vanished forever from the world of the mortals. He did not mention in vain, at one time, that it was going to be very hard to have in Athens another Socrates, with the mission of questioning his friends and strangers, concerned with trying to make them better in the things that truly transcend the soul and that are used to achieve wisdom, or attempt to acquire it, and by those that we shall be judged for at the end of time. Regardless of everything and against all darkness, his light reaches us; similar to the stars of the universe of whom we receive their rays of light, even though the emitting body no longer exists.

Son of a sculptor and midwife, he felt closer to his mother; he said: "I also help give birth to others. Not children, but ideas". This emanated that he was a man that first looked inside his self. He defined himself as a gadfly or wasp; since his habit of scrutinizer of souls and others did not give peace to anyone.

I WILL BE THANKFUL IF YOU REFUTE ME AND LIBERATE ME FROM MY EXTRAVAGANCES. DO NOT STOP FROM QUESTIONING ME, PLEASE, SHOW ME THAT I AM NOT CORRECT.

SOCRATES
From the year 469 to 399 BCE.